THE BRIDGE PLUS ANNUAL

Edited by

Elena Jeronimidis

First published 1991 by Mr Bridge Limited
Ryden Grange, Limecroft Road, Bisley, Surrey

Distributed by Milestone Publications
62 Murray Road, Horndean, Hampshire

Edited by Elena Jeronimidis
Illustrated by Elizabeth and Tom Heydeman, Elena Jeronimidis, Martin Goode and Hedwig Alting von Geusau

Typeset by Best Impressions, Farnham Common, Buckinghamshire
Printed in Great Britain by Ashford Colour Press, Gosport, Hampshire

ISBN   1 85265 122 9

CONTENTS

SPEAKING PERSONALLY

Last year, THE BRIDGE PLUS ANNUAL – our first – was well received. The enjoyment of bridge which its pages wanted to capture touched a chord in readers and critics alike. In fact everybody was generous with praise and we received no criticism – constructive or otherwise – that might have helped to make this, our second Annual, a better publication. The re-appraisal has come entirely from within the editorial team, and we hope that our efforts will meet with your approval.

I am, however, indebted to those who described our first Annual as 'a compilation of the best of BRIDGE PLUS', for giving me the opportunity to state that our Annuals are no such thing. All the articles they contain are original – at least, as far as I know!

The articles included in this year's Annual come, once again, from players of all ages (from 15 to over 90) and all standards, amateurs as well as top professionals. THE BRIDGE PLUS ANNUAL is intended to be a fun read which brings together all the organisations and all the people who make the world of bridge so wonderful. This favourite game of ours means different things to each of us, but I believe that the pleasure derived from it is increased by being shared with other people, regardless of their playing standard.

This belief represents the basic philosophy underlying both the ANNUAL and BRIDGE PLUS, and it seems to appeal to many more players than one would think. Thanks to the support of subscribers and advertisers, our magazine is now about to enter its third year, and it continues to develop. We have increased from thirty-two to forty-four pages (without any rise in the subscription cost), and the enthusiasm and the number of our subscribers have grown too.

If you are not already one of us, I hope that by the time you have read THE BRIDGE PLUS ANNUAL you will have joined our merry band. Do bear in mind, however, that as long as you enjoy your bridge – whether you are a subscriber or not – I should like to hear from you. There is next year's Annual to think of – and BRIDGE PLUS is always on the look-out for fresh, new voices.

BROTHER AELRED'S TEXT-BOOK PLAY

by David Bird

"Where do we go now?" grunted the Abbot, levering himself to his feet. Whoever invented these Howell movements deserved to be locked away. A Mitchell made much more sense; he could spend the whole evening in his favourite North seat, at Table 7 by the fire.

Brother Xavier studied the movement card. "We go to Table 4 East-West, Abbot," he replied. "It's in the far corner, I think."

The Abbot's mood was improved when he saw Brother Aelred and his partner awaiting them at Table 4. If the bridge world had a more welcoming sight to offer, he had yet to witness it.

"How are you two doing?" enquired the Abbot, wedging himself into the East seat.

"No better than usual," replied Brother Aelred. "I haven't picked up a good hand all night. You can't do well at a pairs when the opponents play all the hands."

No, thought the Abbot; not when you defend like Brother Aelred and Brother Michael, anyway.

Brother Aelred's run of poor hands was brought to an end by the hand opposite. The Abbot, to his right, opened 3♣. Brother Aelred thought back to a text-book he had been reading the previous evening. When a pre-empt is made against you, it had said, you should compete against it on the assumption that your partner has 8 points.

South
♠ A K Q J 10 8
♡ A K Q
♢ A 7 5 4
♣ —

Right, thought Brother Aelred, if partner has 8 points they're likely to be ♢K-Q-J and perhaps ♣Q. In that case a grand slam should be on. There seemed to be a flaw in that reasoning, though. Surely Brother Xavier, the Abbot's partner, was just as likely to hold these cards as Brother Michael was. Perhaps the 8-point rule didn't apply when you held 23 points yourself.

Brother Aelred decided to be conservative. "Six spades," he said.

There was no further bidding and the ♣9 was led. Brother Michael, with a slightly mischievous expression, laid out the dummy:

"I hope that's what you were looking for," he said.

North
♠ 6 2
♡ 9 8 5 2
♢ 10 6 3
♣ 10 5 4

Brother Aeldred gave a disbelieving shake of the head. The book had promised 8 points in the dummy, not a complete Yarborough. "Small club, please," he said.

"No, no, wait!" exclaimed Brother Michael. "I've only put down twelve cards. I have the Ace of clubs for you."

Brother Aelred sighed heavily. "Most of us gave up feeble jokes like that when we left prep school," he declared. "OK, play the Ace, then."

The Abbot leaned forward. "The small card is already played; you can't change it now," he said. "Not that I want to benefit personally, of course, but I don't believe rules should be deliberately flouted."

This was the full deal:

Brother Aelred ruffed the club in the South hand and drew trumps in three rounds. For want of anything better to do, he then cashed his heart honours, finding the suit 3–3. The cards below were still out:

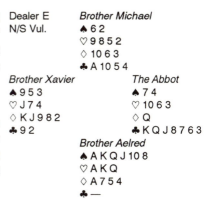

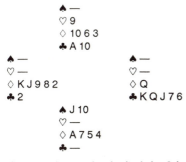

Brother Aelred thought back to the learned text-book he had read the previous night. Obviously the section on bidding was unreliable . . . 8 points in the dummy – he'd never heard such nonsense. Perhaps the section on play was better. He remembered reading that when a contract seemed hopeless you should always duck a round of something. You had to . . . what was it . . . ah, yes, you had to 'register the count'. Not that he had the faintest idea what it meant.

Deciding to give the recommended technique a try, Brother Aelred exited with a low diamond. The Abbot, East, could not believe it when he won with the bare Queen and had to return a club. Thanks to the inspired duck at trick one, Brother Aelred could now win the club return in dummy. One diamond loser went away on this trick and the other on the thirteenth heart. Against all the odds the slam had been made.

"Now, how many down was that?" enquired Brother Michael, who had not followed the play since the apparent disaster at trick one.

"I made it, I think," replied Brother Aelred. "I believe I just lost one diamond."

Brother Xavier looked helplessly at the Abbot. "It's no good if I put in the King of diamonds," he said. "Your Queen falls, and I have to lead away from the Jack."

The Abbot gave a bleak nod of the head and turned towards Brother Aelred. "Did you have the faintest idea what you were doing there?" he demanded.

"It's an amazing coincidence, but I was reading about that very play only yesterday," replied Brother Aelred. "I'll lend you the book, if you like."

The Abbot muttered something under his breath.

"Mind you, I shouldn't bother with the section on bidding," continued Brother Aelred. He gave a sad shake of the head. "No, it's very unsound."

CONVENTIONAL WEAR
by Smart Alec

In the old days, nobody would have dreamt of playing bridge unless dressed in the smartest attire. Alas, times have changed, and formal dress has taken second place to Master Points in today's list of priorities. However, there is no reason why casual wear should not be tasteful, and the following recommendations from a top *couturier* will provide helpful guidelines.

Portly gentlemen in their fifties, who enjoy nothing more than a beer with their post-mortems, should choose low-cut trousers that can be belted up underneath their stomachs, and tailored shirts (preferably one size too small) which burst open between each button to reveal large portions of hairy chests.

Ladies in their thirties, who aspire to being noted for their bridge prowess rather than their sex-appeal, should adopt an androgynous fashion that but hints at their femininity. Men's dirty jeans, preferably bought at a supermarket, and equally dirty sweat-shirts should be their standard attire. This should not be spoiled by any head-dress, although it is recommended that they wash their hair before a bridge session. Unclean trainers, on the other hand, are *de rigueur*.

A gentleman keen on making an impression on the opposite sex should cultivate an intellectual image, which might enable him to achieve good results. A casual suede jacket, a neckerchief, and chequered trousers are enhanced by a pipe. Hair should be worn long (this might also help in concealing balding patches), and spectacles assist in giving an overall impression of intense mental activity.

For the lady no longer in her first bloom, we recommend youthful frocks and all her jewels, so as to convey an aura of assurance. Hair should be worn short and blow-dried in the latest style, handbag and shoes should match. There is nothing like exuding self-confidence to achieve good results at the bridge table!

TOP OF NOTHING
by Geoffrey Breskal

It was Wednesday night and although it was my day off, I had arranged to play with one of our newer members in the 25p per 100 partnership game. The snow was falling heavily, but in spite of road conditions I managed to get to St. John's Wood Bridge Club on time.

After exchanging pleasantries we decided that our system would be 'Bubble and Squeak'. To people who do not live within the sound of Bow Bells, the former means Double for Take-out over pre-empts, and the latter stands for Weak No-trump throughout.

On the first hand, the opposition bid to 3NT after Stayman over the 15–17 no-trump opener by South. My partner led the ◊9. I saw no future in this suit, and decided that the best chance was to switch to the ♣10, hoping to make three club tricks and two Aces. As you can see, declarer only had to knock out my ♡A to claim nine tricks, which he duly did.

My partner immediately berated me for not leading back his suit. I defended myself by inquiring why he had led the *nine* of diamonds. "Top of Nothing," he replied. "But you had the Jack," I retorted.

His reply, "Call *that* Something!" ended the discussion.

	North	
	♠ K J 7 4	
	♡ K J 8	
	◊ 10 8 3	
	♣ 6 3 2	
West		East
♠ 6 5 3		♠ 10 9 2
♡ 9 4 2		♡ A 7 5
◊ J 9 6 4 2		◊ A Q 5
♣ K Q		♣ 10 9 8 7
	South	
	♠ A Q 8	
	♡ Q 10 6 3	
	◊ K 7	
	♣ A J 5 4	

MURPHY'S LAW
by Graham Hazel

At this point in the play I must stop.
Should I try the finesse or the drop?
But I don't delay long,
For I'll always guess wrong,
And score a clear bottom (not top)!

BRIDGE HOLIDAYS –
ARE THEY FOR ME?

by Mike Swanson

Everyone knows that you need to be a little crazy to play bridge, but even some of the most enthusiastic players think that the idea of spending hundreds of pounds to go to the sun, and then staying indoors to play a game that could just as easily be played at home, is an act of complete lunacy!

Who actually does indulge in this type of activity? It is difficult to describe a typical bridge holiday client, but I shall have a go. She (the ladies usually outnumber the men two to one) is probably around about retirement age and of average playing standard. There is always a sprinkling of players in their thirties and forties on the holidays, but those who have young children or who are linked to education are unlikely to be found on bridge holidays because the trips tend to take place on the fringe of the season during term time.

Let me clear up another fallacy – they do *not* stay indoors and play cards all day. There is bridge available late afternoon (typically 3.15 to 5.30) where the 'bridge-aholics' can always be found, but many clients only venture into the bridge room for the evening sessions which run from 8.30 to 11.30. The rest of the time everyone does their own thing, from sunbathing to hiking. I am actually writing this article whilst running a bridge holiday in Austria, *(at the hotel pictured below)* and the clients have amazed me with their energy; I have been exhausted just listening to such comments as 'We have just returned from an eight-mile walk up the mountain' or 'I set my alarm for 6.15 a.m. so that I would not miss the bus to Salzburg'. To me, those comments sound more like excursions into the world of masochism than those of people enjoying a relaxing holiday!

Diamond Bridge in Austria

If you are single, then a bridge holiday should rate very highly indeed; most tour operators welcome singles and guarantee a partner for all bridge sessions (we always carry a spare person who will only play if needed as do other bridge holiday organisers). Another bonus is that there are always people around with whom you have an interest in common, so it is easy to strike up a conversation by the pool with opening gambits such as 'What did you do last night on the hand with the nine-card diamond suit?' or 'Do you know what my partner did to me on hand 23?'

Running bridge holidays is such a wecome contrast for me in my tournament-directing capacity – the only calls for the director relate to opening leads out of turn or revokes; there are no nasty hesitation incidents or accusations of sharp practice; after all, first and foremost people are on holiday and the bridge, although still important, does not become as tense as it often seems at congresses.

On days involving the 'compulsory' long excursions, the bridge at the end of the evening becomes riddled with tired mistakes as players fight to stay awake. I have learned to end the bridge around 11.30 p.m., even if not many boards have been played, as if one looks around the room at that time there seem to be more yawns than bids.

At the end of one such evening in Austria a defender nearly revoked, but noticed just in time and ended up with a trump as a major penalty card; later on in the hand she ruffed with the penalty card and immediately led a card of the suit she had just ruffed! Such things are not unusual on a bridge holiday – fortunately, since it was a holiday, the offender's husband was able to laugh about it. I doubt that he would react in the same light-hearted manner away from the holiday environment!

At the end of most holidays we finish up with a Gala Dinner including local entertainment and dancing. Sometimes the clients get together to put on their own cabaret; such was the case in Tenerife recently, when the 'Diamond Girls' *(in the photograph)* put together and presented their very own 'Bridge Holiday Rap.'

Talking about the Gala Dinner brings me to the one aspect of the holiday which I fear. I mentioned earlier that the ladies outnumber the men about two to one, and this creates a problem when it comes to the dancing. Somehow it seems to be expected that the Tournament Director should get up and dance in order to help redress the balance. My business colleague, Carol Yates, hates cards as much as I hate dancing but said that she would learn to play bridge if I learnt to dance (equally she loves to dance as much as I enjoy bridge), so both of us have endured lessons and become proficient in each other's interests.

I can hear you asking: 'If she hates cards, why is she involved in bridge holidays?' That's a long story – perhaps Carol will tell you in next year's ANNUAL!

See you on a bridge holiday sometime?

FIXING THE OPPONENTS
by Glyn Liggins

Glyn Liggins is the Editor of

Maxwell Macmillan
BRIDGE

London Road, Wheatley
Oxford OX9 1YR

"You are not going to be right against pre-empts more than 60-65% of the time. You have to accept that occasionally you will be fixed."
(Mike Lawrence)

We have all encountered a situation where we have passed a pre-empt, when action from either side of the table would be too aggressive, only to find that we can make a game. Alternatively, the impertinence of the opposition has driven us to make a bid that we would not be proud to show to our mothers, and we have ended up overboard. Pre-empts are a very dangerous weapon – that is why the notion has survived since bridge was in its infancy. They create problems for the opposition and, more than anything, they are great fun to play.

The next step in the logic is the one you are going to find hard to swallow. If pre-empting is such a problem-poser for the opposition, why don't we increase the possibility of our taking such an action? And when we do, why don't we make it likely that the opponents are missing out on something? You know what's coming, don't you?

When the vulnerability is favourable to your side, be prepared to open with a pre-empt on hands that most people would not think twice about. Let's consider some examples. Try this hand from the England trials.

Liggins	Dyson
♠ J	♠ A K 10 9 8 6
♡ 8 5 3	♡ Q 10 6
◇ 10 8 4	◇ —
♣ 9 8 6 5 3 2	♣ A K J 10

As West, I opened 3♣ and partner raised to 5♣. No problem!

Can you imagine the biggest possible penalty double of a Weak-Two bid? How about holding: ♠ A K Q 9 2 ♡ A K Q J ◇ A 8 4 2 ♣ Void over a weak 2♠ bid? Richard Fleet had this problem in the Spring Foursomes of 1991. He was playing double for take out! The full hand is shown at the top of the opposite page.

South	West	North	East	
2♠ (a)	NB (b)	NB	3♣	(a) Weak
NB	3NT (c)	All Pass		(b) What else can you do?
				(c) See (b)

	Dyson	Dealer: South
	♠ J	E/W Vul.
	♡ 10 7 5 3	
	♢ K Q 10 3	
	♣ 9 7 4 2	

Fleet		Durmus
♠ A K Q 9 2		♠ 8 4
♡ A K Q J		♡ 9 8 6 2
♢ A 8 4 2		♢ 5
♣ —		♣ A K Q 10 8 3

	Liggins	
	♠ 10 7 6 5 3	
	♡ 4	
	♢ J 9 7 6	
	♣ J 6 5	

Despite holding eight tricks in his own hand, Fleet went down in 3NT, with 6♡ a very good contract as the cards are. It was a flat board, because unfortunately my team-mates went astray in 6♡ in the other room.

A few words of warning:

1) Make sure that you explain your weird tendencies on the convention card.

2) Make sure that partner is on the same wavelength – you don't want him leaping to 6NT on such as:
♠ A K x ♡ A K x ♢ A x x x ♣ A x x
over your 3♣ bid, only to find that not even 3NT is playable.

3) Play with tolerant team-mates.

4) Have a sense of humour!

The last is very important because occasionally this kind of thing happens:

West	North	East	South
3♣	NB	NB	Dbl
All Pass			

No doubt if declarer plays very carefully he can guarantee two tricks, but my partner was not up to it! He made one trick for a penalty of minus 2000 and a loss of 11 IMPS. Team-mates, bless their hearts, just laughed.

All this is not for the feeble-hearted, but it is great fun to play.

	North	Dealer: West
	♠ K 5	N/S Vul.
	♡ A 5	
	♢ A 9 3 2	
	♣ A K 10 8 6	

West		East
♠ 7 4 3		♠ 10 9 8
♡ 9 8		♡ J 7 4 3 2
♢ Q 5		♢ J 10 6 4
♣ J 9 7 5 3 2		♣ 4

	South	
	♠ A Q J 6 2	
	♡ K Q 10 6	
	♢ K 8 7	
	♣ Q	

13

A RUBBER TO REMEMBER
by Tony Richards

Bridge players tend to remember their bad luck far more than their good. We either don't notice our good fortune or take it for granted.

The following hands – the biggest rubber in two hands that I have ever won – owed everything to good fortune. They occurred in an undergraduate rubber evening, at a penny a hundred (1d that is, not 1p) but one can win or lose the price of an evening's drinking even at that stake, and of course there is always the matter of prestige.

At Love All, dealer South, the bidding (North-South silent throughout) went: 1NT – 4NT – 6NT!

West	East
♠ 8 5 4	♠ K J 6
♡ K Q 9 5	♡ A J 8 7
◇ J 7	◇ A K 4
♣ A K 9 8	♣ J 7 6

No excuses for the bidding – it was just youthful exuberance and the frustration of a losing run.

Trying to sound cheerful, I thanked partner and made a token effort to make this ludicrous contract. The heart lead was won in hand, and a spade played to the Jack – it held! The ♣J was covered by the Queen and Ace, and a second spade led to the King. Three more rounds of hearts were played ending in dummy, South discarding two diamonds and a club. It now only remained to finesse against the ♣10 and make the slam. To find four finesses right has a probability of just 6.25%.

This was the very next hand. With North-South (yet again!) silent throughout, the bidding went:

West	East
2♡	3◇
3♡	4♣
4◇	6◇
7◇	

North — Dealer: West, E/W now Vul.
♠ Q J 5 3
♡ Q J 6 4
◇ Q 9
♣ 9 8 3

West	East
♠ A	♠ 9 6 4
♡ A K 10 9 8 7 2	♡ 3
◇ 8 5 3	◇ A K J 7 4
♣ A 2	♣ K J 10 4

South
♠ K 10 8 7 2
♡ 5
◇ 10 6 2
♣ Q 7 6 5

I still think the seventh heart makes the West hand an Acol-two opener, but the last two bids are definitely 'exuberant'. East said it was obvious that we were headed for a slam, so he might as well bid it; West thought there must be a good diamond suit opposite, and that his controls and the heart suit would make the slam an easy make. And so it proved, for South, remembering an old adage about safe leads against grand slams, led a trump! After drawing trumps declarer has just enough trumps left in hand – and entries in dummy – to establish and run the hearts.

After this the fortunes turned back again and we didn't win another rubber, but I'm sure I must be due for some more good luck again soon.

BRIDGE MY WAY
by Zia Mahmood

I was twenty-two years old, and I had just returned home to Pakistan. The social scene for the young was rather limited there. At the time, I was trying to get better acquainted with an attractive girl whom I knew only slightly. The good news was that she finally agreed to meet me. The bad news was that the venue was a bridge party! It wasn't my idea of a perfect date, as I couldn't even play bridge, but it was better than nothing.

I had, of course, told my date that I could play. To try and avoid looking too foolish, I picked up a book, Alfred Sheinwold's *Five Weeks to Winning Bridge*. I hoped I could compress five weeks into just three days. Much to my surprise, I found the book interesting. The big day arrived and, as you can imagine, I performed embarrassingly – but managed to save myself from a position of indecent exposure. But I was sufficiently intrigued by the game that my concentration diverted from my reason for being there, the girl, to the intricacies of the game itself.

That was almost the last I saw of her. My mind became enthralled; the spark had been lit, and soon became a fire. No, not a fire, more like a furnace. Over the next few months I read all the bridge books I could lay my hands on. My intention was to learn the rules and techniques, but at the same time I was introduced to the fascinating people inhabiting the world of bridge. At that time, it never occurred to me that many of those people would become my friends, some even my partners.

Two books stick vividly in my mind. *Right Through the Pack*, by Robert Darvas and Norman de Villiers Hart, a charming fairy-tale collection of bridge hands; and Terence Reese's *Play Bridge with Reese*. I have read both of them many times, and recommend them unreservedly.

Hooked, I started to play with a group of friends. Like all beginners, I experienced mostly frustration. I would finally master one point, only to find that there were many others to learn and conquer. But I remember the pleasure, the mixture of pride and satisfaction, after making a good play – a feeling no non-bridge player can understand. I was determined not just to learn the game, but to master it and become good. I was in a hurry, too, which didn't help. But learning was such fun that the time flew by painlessly, and I started to improve.

Non-bridge players, scared of taking up the game, always protest, 'I'm sure you must be very good with numbers!' or, 'I'm too old to learn.' Neither could be further from the truth. While playing you might need to count to thirteen, which everyone has been able to do since they were one or two years old. The only tough calculation I ever have to do is after the game, when I have to add up how much money I've won or lost on the day. As for age, well – I started to learn the game at twenty-two. I had never even thought about bridge before. If you have a talent, age isn't that important.

Having mentioned talent, just what qualities or talents are required by a bridge player? Which type of person does well at the game?

These are tough questions to answer. To try to uncover the truth, I asked fifty of the world's best players to give me one word to describe a top bridge player. What did I find out? Nothing! Or, more accurately, the answers varied so much that it appears nobody has any real idea. Here are some of the words they came up with: imagination, intensity, concentration, talent, judgement, stamina, logic, focused, aware, card-sense, desire to win (some people just can't count!), technique, determination, creativity, quickness of thought, discipline, dedication, consistency, psychology, relaxed, confident – enough already.

In other words, anything and everything. I don't think there is anyone who wouldn't identify with at least one of these, probably several. Still, it is interesting to note that not one person mentioned mathematics in any shape or form.

The best players are so varied in their personalities and characteristics. All sorts of people can succeed in bridge; there is no stereotype for the perfect player. Answering my own question, I think these are the three most important talents:

   1) a logical and clear-thinking mind;   2) card-sense;   3) a positive attitude.

There is one more thing: a trait rather than a talent. I have found that most top players have enormous egos. I am no exception in this respect – and in my case it's actually warranted. My excuse, if I need one, is that it's necessary to remain strong and confident in one's own ability to stay at the top.

Anyway, after about six months of fanatical playing and reading, regularly falling asleep at work, and being ostracised and abused by non-bridge playing friends, things were improving. I can still recall the afternoon when I played a hand that reduced to this 3-card ending:

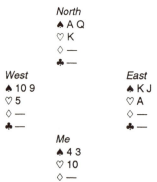

I was just about to take the spade finesse when somewhere a light dawned. I led the ♡10, endplaying East to lead away from the ♠K.

Looking back now, it's no big deal. But at the time I was euphoric, I relived the play in my mind time and again, and couldn't wait for another chance to execute an endplay.

I suppose that was the point of no return. From that moment the game had me; I was addicted.

This is an abridged excerpt from Zia Mahmood's autobiography, Bridge My Way, *shortly to be published by Faber & Faber.*

EVERYTHING IN ITS PLACE

by Dave Huggett

It is a strange fact of life that bridge players who are graduating from the role of beginner to a more elevated status have an almost perfect memory when it comes to bad habits. Now this may well be due to the fact that in an untutored mind it is much more simple *from the teacher's point of view* to issue a set of well-defined rules to cover most elementary bidding and play problems – much like playing bridge by numbers – but the danger arises, of course, in taking rules as ends in themselves. In other words, they act as a substitute for good, honest, intellectual toil! It would be rather absurd to suggest that bridge is not a game of the mind, in just the same way as one would not expect a chess player to sit down and move the pieces at random, in the faint hope that it might work out well. Rules are fine, up to a point, but everything should be kept in its place.

East knew all about the rules on the following hand and followed them faithfully – much to his partner's chagrin. With East-West silent throughout, the bidding had not taken long:

South	North
1NT	2♣
2◊	3NT

North
♠ K Q J
♡ A 8 5 4
◊ Q J
♣ Q J 9 6

East
♠ 10 2
♡ J 10 7 3
◊ 10 7 6 2
♣ K 5 3

"Don't make too many tricks," quipped North after his partner had opened a weak no-trump and had been raised to game when no major fit came to light. West led the ♠7, won in dummy, and declarer immediately led the ♣Q. Now East knew all about this type of situation and remembering his teacher's stern advice about covering honours, he played low with a warm feeling inside. What he should have done, of course, was to have thought along the following lines:

1) My partner has at least five spades to the Ace, because of the Stayman denial and the Rule of Eleven.

2) Apart from the ♠A my partner can have at most four other points.

3) Unless he holds the ♣A there is no hope of beating this contract.

North
♠ K Q J
♡ A 8 5 4
◊ Q J
♣ Q J 9 6

Accordingly, East should have ignored the rule he had learnt so assiduously and risen with the ♣K to play back his remaining spade.

Declarer would have struggled for a few minutes, then conceded defeat.

The full deal was as shown.

West
♠ A 9 8 7 3
♡ 6 2
◊ 8 5 4 3
♣ A 7

East
♠ 10 2
♡ J 10 7 3
◊ 10 7 6 2
♣ K 5 3

South
♠ 6 5 4
♡ K Q 9
◊ A K 9
♣ 10 8 4 2

It was another kind of rule altogether that East could not bring himself to break on the next hand, although with a little foresight the right answer should have been apparent.

East was delighted with his hand on this occasion, and opened 1♡, but was disturbed when South made a weak jump overcall in spades which North meanly raised to game. In deference to his bidding, West led the ♡2 which was won with the Ace by East, who returned the ♡6. Declarer won with the King and played a spade to the Jack and Ace – and now East sat and pondered. What would *you* have done now? Well, the answer of course is 'nothing',

North
♠ Q J 7 2
♡ 10 9 4
♢ K Q J 10
♣ A Q

East
♠ A 4
♡ A Q 8 6
♢ A 8 4
♣ K 9 3 2

because the opportunity has already passed you by. It is imperative that partner should gain the lead to push a club through dummy while the ♢A is still intact, and the only entry partner can have is the ♡J. Accordingly, East should play the Queen at trick one – furnishing that entry and paving the way for declarer's defeat. Not difficult really, just a question of being on your toes. The full hand was as opposite.

North
♠ Q J 7 2
♡ 10 9 4
♢ K Q J 10
♣ A Q

West
♠ 5
♡ J 5 3 2
♢ 9 3 2
♣ 8 7 6 5 4

East
♠ A 4
♡ A Q 8 6
♢ A 8 4
♣ K 9 3 2

South
♠ K 10 9 8 6 3
♡ K 7
♢ 7 6 5
♣ J 10

It was West on the final hand who did scant justice to his little grey cells, and while this time declarer could have countered the manoeuvre, there was a good chance that he would have gone wrong.

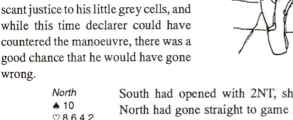

North
♠ 10
♡ 8 6 4 2
♢ A J 10 9 6
♣ 9 6 2

West
♠ Q J 9 8 6
♡ 9 5
♢ K 8 4
♣ 10 7 4

South had opened with 2NT, showing 20–22 points, and North had gone straight to game in that strain, ignoring the possible heart fit. West had an easy lead of the ♠Q, and when this was ducked he continued confidently with another. Declarer won and led a small diamond to the Jack and Queen, won the spade return and successfully repeated the diamond finesse. Completely in charge, declarer claimed ten tricks, but yet again a golden opportunity had gone begging. West had been conditioned to play 'second hand low', and had not even considered the possibility of playing the ♢K when declarer had initially led that suit. Consider what might have happened if he had: placing West with both the King

```
          North
          ♠ 10
          ♡ 8 6 4 2
          ◇ A J 10 9 6
          ♣ 9 6 2
West                      East
♠ Q J 9 8 6               ♠ 7 5 4 2
♡ 9 5                     ♡ Q J 10 3
◇ K 8 4                   ◇ Q 3
♣ 10 7 4                  ♣ Q J 5
          South
          ♠ A K 3
          ♡ A K 7
          ◇ 7 5 2
          ♣ A K 8 3
```

and Queen of diamonds, declarer might well have ducked the King and taken a subsequent losing finesse to East's now bare Queen – to the delight of the defenders and his own mortification. The full hand was as opposite.

Dave Huggett

PAIN IN THE NECK
by David Lawton

Some innocent activities, occupational and sporting, are hazardous to health but carry no printed warning. There's housemaid's knee and tennis elbow, whereas golfers and gardeners risk backache. This is well documented, but my claim to fame is that I have identified an ailment afflicting one exclusive group.

It is 'Bridgeplayer's Neck': a chronic sprain induced by staring at the ceiling in bridge clubs. Clubs come in all shapes and sizes (like their members) but have one thing in common: a magical ceiling engraved with invisible writing.

Acolytes have eyes that bring the symbols to light. They stare upward to discern if partner's bid is a slam try – or is he drunk? The ceiling will tell all.

On hearing your response to his Directional Asking Bid, partner looks up in search of guidance. He sits entranced, lips moving in silent prayer or curses. Your opponents covertly follow his gaze, seemingly unconcerned. The ceiling looks bare to them (they are Blue Club players) and somewhat in need of repair. The moments pass, each one more slowly. Opponents now activate Operation Seat Shuffling and Throat Clearing. This is in subdued manner (no clear evidence of discourtesy) but their patience is tested, and you know it and wonder what your partner's problem can be because any idiot must know what your bid meant.

Partner is unaware of the atmosphere at the table: it is beneath him. He is in the rarefied stratosphere, staring at the emulsioned plaster as though it were Michelangelo's masterpiece. Suddenly, the mist clears from his eyes; he has seen the light. He lowers his head abruptly, and you all hear the ominous click. He winces. Another victim of Bridgeplayer's Neck.

Partner announces his rebid. Your eyes pop. Is he determined to give you an ulcer? Your head jerks up. You stare at the ceiling . . .

MAKE YOUR PARTNER A BETTER PLAYER

John Barr

Hi! I've written this article just for you. I've seen you at the club a few times, and you strike me as being a very good player. Despite that, you never seem to do very well. It's most frustrating, isn't it? There are two main reasons for your lack of success. Firstly, you are unbelievably unlucky. Whenever you bid a grand slam the Ace of trumps is always offside, always. Secondly, your partner is rubbish. You only agreed to play with him as a favour when his previous partner left the country at rather short notice. You thought it was just for the evening, perhaps a week or two – that was sixteen years ago. Ever since, you have been squirming in your seat as partner passed your forcing bids, butchered solid contracts, and trumped your Aces with master trumps.

There's not much you can do about it. Some people (like Belladonna, Forrester and our esteemed Editor) are born lucky. Others (like you and me) must continually suffer the slings and arrows of outrageous fortune – and partner. On the brighter side there are several things you can do about your partner. You can shoot him. (Whilst this solves one problem it creates another which the police feel is rather more serious.) You could emigrate to Bolivia and strike up a new partnership with your partner's previous partner. (This option tends to play havoc with your social life, and the daily commuting to Paddington would be even more unbearable.)

This seems to leave you with only one recourse. You will have to make partner a better player! Now, you have proved that partner will never really improve no matter how many books he reads, or how many hours you waste on system discussions. What you will have to do is make life easier for partner at the table. Before you make a bid that is at all obscure, ask yourself if its meaning could be correctly deduced by a single-cell amœba. If the answer is yes, then partner will at least have an evens chance of getting it right. On a good day. And you know how often he has those.

As I am writing this article for THE BRIDGE PLUS ANNUAL as opposed to the Journal of Psychology, I suppose I should include a hand.

Responder	Opener	RHO	Responder	LHO
♠ A K	1♡	NB	4◊	Dbl
♡ Q x x x x				
◊ Q J x x x	5◊	NB	?	
♣ K				

Opener bids 1♡, to which the reponse is 4◇, showing a good raise to 4♡, but denying two Aces and a feature. Next hand doubles and opener rebids 5◇. What does this bid mean? It's obviously encouraging, and as your opponent has advertised diamond values it must surely show a void. Now, if opener held the ♣A would he bypass 5♣? Probably not. You have the ♠A, so why is opener so enthusiastic?

The only answer is that together with the diamond void and nothing much in the black suits opener must have great trumps. So the bid is obvious – 6♡. Left-hand opponent, with the ◇A-K and the ♣A (and having seen your slam bidding before) doubles, and when it comes back to you the redouble seems pretty automatic. The obvious (?) diamond is led, and partner wraps up all thirteen tricks.

So, what's the point of this hand? It's the 5◇ bid. I showed the hand to a number of 'experts', and they all redoubled. The other hand is shown below.

Opener
♠ Q x x
♡ A K x x x x
◇ —
♣ Q x x x

The amœba, your partner

After 4◇ is doubled opener knows that responder cannot have many wasted values in that suit, and the 5◇ bid tells the whole story of his hand (diamond void, no black-suit Ace, therefore great trumps). The redouble might well be technically correct, but it has two drawbacks. First, it only tells partner about one feature in the hand, when one has the opportunity to tell the whole story in one bid. Secondly, one looks pretty stupid going nine off in 4◇ redoubled when 6♡ is cold. I know, I have been there in the regional final of the aggregate-scored Hubert Phillips competition. (That ex-partner emigrated to America.)

By now I suppose you will be full of admiration for not only the logic behind the 5◇ bid, but also my speed of thought in finding it at the table. Well, I have a confession to make. I didn't bid 5◇ . . . that was my partner!

WARNING

by Alistair Flutter

My new partner has plenty to fear,
He's my seventh in less than a year.
For the higher the stakes,
The worse the mistakes,
I just can't get my brain into gear!

WHAT'S LURKING?

by Hey

The drawing below contains ten images which illustrate the names of ten bridge *Coups*. Can you find them all? *(Solution on page 127.)*

TO BOLDLY GO . . .

by Keith Roberts

Light overcalls, just as much as light opening bids, are the very essence of aggressive and successful Match-pointed Pairs bidding and play. For instance, consider this hand which was dealt on a bridge holiday where I was directing. At Game All, West, the dealer, opened 1♠ and North surveyed the collection below.

North	
♠	A K J 7 4 2
♡	—
◇	10 9 7 5 3
♣	5 3

What would you do in North's position? Many chose to pass, awaiting further developments on what appeared to be a misfit between the opposing partnership. Others thought it more likely that East-West might find a fit in hearts if left to their own devices, and imaginatively bid 2◇ on a somewhat meagre holding.

Their boldness paid off when East passed and South gleefully surveyed this hand.

South	
♠	3
♡	Q 6
◇	A K Q J 2
♣	A 10 8 6 2

South's glee, however, is to be short-lived, for it is not obvious what the best bid is in the circumstances. A pre-emptive 5◇? The hand is far too strong for that. Then why not go straight to six? But what about the two losing hearts?

Try Blackwood – but if one Ace is shown, which one is it? Why not mark time by cue-bidding the spade suit to seek more information about North's hand?

West did not let this go unchallenged and, as feared, bid the heart suit at the 3-level.

Back to North's hand. A natural 3♠ or a conventional 4♡ kept the pot boiling, but did not stop East supporting West's hearts at the 4- or 5-level. This was sufficient for either side to consider a slam a realistic prospect.

Incidentally, all is not lost should North choose to pass rather than overcall 2◇ at the first opportunity. Whether East passes or bids 2♡, South can call upon the old faithful 2NT to ask for the better minor, and North's emphatic 5◇ bid over any call West makes guarantees a fight for the slam call.

As you can see, North-South make 6◇ for the loss of one club. East-West lose a trick in each side suit (plus a possible overruff on a second round of spades after a spade lead) to go two or three down in 6♡. Not a bad sacrifice, especially at pairs!

	North	
	♠ A K J 7 4 2	
	♡ —	
	◇ 10 9 7 5 3	
	♣ 5 3	
West		*East*
♠ Q 10 9 8 6		♠ 5
♡ A K J 10 7		♡ 9 8 5 4 3 2
◇ 6 4		◇ 8
♣ 4		♣ K Q J 9 7
	South	
	♠ 3	
	♡ Q 6	
	◇ A K Q J 2	
	♣ A 10 8 6 2	

COLLECTING PLAYING CARDS
by Merle Jarrett

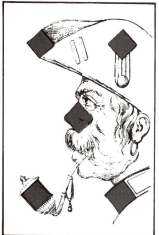

Collecting is fashionable, and as expensive or cheap, and as time and space-consuming, as you choose. Old playing cards are regarded by bridge players as rubbish to be thrown away as soon as they become dirty. Luckily, in the past, not everyone has felt that way, and it is still possible to find antiquarian (as opposed to just 'old') playing cards.

My own interest stemmed from an article in the *Birmingham Post* which opened my eyes to the history and diversity of playing cards. Since I read it several years ago, I have spent many happy hours visiting antique shops and fairs. Not that I have always been successful; in fact, the biggest problem was getting started.

My first 'pack' had only thirteen cards (I wonder what happened to the other three hands!) and to obtain the second I had to buy, at what seemed like great cost, the beautiful card box that housed it. This gave rise to the collection of anything connected with playing cards – but I digress. The advantage of collecting cards is that it is easy to specialise – in a country, a period, a

manufacturer, advertising packs, or even Jokers (you'd be astonished at the diversity of these, and generally your friends are happy to part with Jokers from their new packs).

Packs of cards have been used not only for card games, but also for fortune-telling, satire, history and geography lessons, to say nothing of children's games: for example, the original Jacques *Happy Families* described as *A new and most diverting game for juveniles* with *Forty-four*

Mrs. Dip the Dyer's Wife.

Mrs. Dip the Dyer's Wife.

INDIRA GANDHI

Grotesque Characters which include *Mrs Bung* the *Brewer's wife* and *Mrs Dip* the *Dyer's wife* as particularly grotesque, all for an original cost of one shilling.

Playing cards probably came to England in the early 15th Century, and they are mentioned in official documents in 1463, 1483, and 1495. Modern English cards are based on the 14th Century 'Rouen' design, and in 1628 the Worshipful Company of Playing Cards Manufacturers was founded by Royal Charter, with complete prohibition of all importation of playing cards into England and Wales being introduced on 1st December 1628. The King, determined not to lose by the arrangement, having lost his revenue from custom duties, put a duty on card manufacturers. The 'Duty Ace' or 'Old Frizzle' or 'Duty Wrapper' remained until the mid-20th Century, having reached 2s 6d a pack in the early 19th Century.

When I started collecting in the early 1970s it was possible to find unusual packs at a reasonable cost, my prize possession being a single-headed pack circa 1830. In the 1980s Stanley Gibbons became interested in the playing card market; this somewhat inflated prices, but they seem to have settled down recently.

By the way, have you ever wondered how players held a hand of cards without indices? We really must thank the person who thought of 'squeezers', putting small numbers in the corners!

A THOUGHTLESS PASS

by Brenda Jones

There was a young lady from Lydd,
Who answered "Two Clubs" with "No bid".
When her partner did tackle
"I thought you played Acol,"
She ran to a cupboard and hid.

THE PORTLAND BOWL FINALS

by Tom Townsend

Should East make 6♣ on a spade lead?

The deal comes from this year's finals of the British Universities Championship. The final was between Cambridge (who had defeated Oxford in the semifinal) and Birkbeck, London (who had survived a late Edinburgh rally to record a single-figure victory). Birkbeck collected an 1100 penalty to level the first set, but could not keep up with the more experienced Cambridge students for another 40 boards, losing by 116.

	North	Dealer: North
	♠ Q 10 8 6	N/S Vul.
	♡ J 10 8 7 6 3	
	◇ J 2	
	♣ 2	

West		East
♠ A K 3 2		♠ J 9
♡ 9 4 2		♡ A Q
◇ K 9 7		◇ 5 4
♣ Q J 10		♣ A K 9 7 6 5 3

	South	
	♠ 7 5 4	
	♡ K 5	
	◇ A Q 10 8 6 3	
	♣ 8 4	

On the above deal from the second set, Birkbeck played in a safe 3NT, making an overtrick. Cambridge stretched to 6♣ in spite of a weak diamond overcall by South. Declarer won the spade lead and began running his clubs, on which North slipped up by letting a spade go, allowing the spades to be ruffed out thus providing a winner to which the ◇K allowed access. This six-card ending would otherwise have arisen:

East will now cash the ♠K and ruff the other spade. South cannot afford a heart discard, since declarer has a good count on the hand, so might shed his lowest diamonds. Unfortunately, declarer can lead a diamond towards dummy, offering South the choice between rising with the Ace (so establishing dummy's holding) and playing low (to be thrown in with the Ace to lead hearts).

	♠ Q 10 8	
	♡ J	
	◇ J 2	
	♣ —	

♠ K 2		♠ J
♡ 2		♡ A Q
◇ K 9 7		◇ 5 4
♣ —		♣ 3

	♠ —	
	♡ K 5	
	◇ A Q 10 8	
	♣ —	

The Cambridge players consoled North with this analysis, and moved on. It was not until several weeks later that the truth of the hand came to light. If South discards both the *Ace* and the *Queen* of diamonds on the spades, then *his partner* will be able to win with the Knave and set the contract with his last spade.

On the other hand, declarer can always make the contract: he wins the opening lead, cashes the ♣A-K, plays two rounds of spades, ruffing, and a club to the Queen to ruff the fourth spade out. Now he runs his trumps and South can no longer avoid the strip-squeeze by throwing the ◇A-Q, as North will have no spade to cash when a diamond is ducked to him.

Not many players would find this line at the table!

BRIDGE TODAY
by Peter Donovan

Peter Donovan writes for the

Daily Mail

Telephone 071- 938 6000

There are various reasons why I'm not enthusiastic about writing articles for bridge magazines – emerging from the safe confines of my daily column into the pages of publications which take themselves, and the game, too seriously. My main gripe is that most bridge features are either boringly subjective and parochially blinkered, or unnecessarily technical – and often a combination of all these. Good bridge writing should be objective or humorous, preferably both. So if I'm going to write subjectively, I'd prefer it to be on topics such as my dislike of French cuisine, the Poll Tax, or sex in the doldrums.

Why, then, am I writing this article for THE BRIDGE PLUS ANNUAL? The praiseworthy efforts of the Editor to produce and sustain a magazine for social players deserve support from all true lovers of the game. I endorse every word she has written when 'Speaking Personally', as I suspect that she shares both my concern about the few destructive elements in the game, and my perspective of the bridge world.

This is broad and simple. My interest lies in *the people* who play the game, rather than the cards they play – or mis-play. So my objective over the past thirty years has been to help others get the same full enjoyment as I derive, from the hobby I love so passionately.

Bridge plays many different roles in people's lives; it is incredible that the same game which gives countless hours of pleasure and social contact to millions, can also provide the ultimate mental challenge and test of endurance for the finest brains. But by far the greatest contribution bridge makes to society is as an antidote for loneliness. Of the many thousands of folk who suddenly find themselves alone each year, a very small proportion had learned to play bridge in former years: they are able to take it up again to find new companionship and preoccupation. I believe that there is another, perhaps much larger proportion, who would welcome and enjoy the camaraderie of the social bridge environment; but the prospect of trying to learn is daunting, when memory has faded a bit and the brain cells are a darker shade of grey. For them, my *Bridge is Still an Easy Game* is not entirely reassuring, for we all know that a fair bit of hard work is necessary to master the basics – but from then on it's just logic, common sense, judgement, and intuition. I've proved, at least to my own satisfaction, that it is as easy to teach the elderly to play as it is to teach children. But children learn more, and more quickly, than adults; so my ideal is that people should be encouraged to learn bridge young – then stash it away for a rainy day.

The National Schools Team Championship which I started in 1965 with the backing of the *Daily Mail* has done a lot to break down the traditional resistance to cards in the classroom. We now have an excellent network of learning facilities for bridge in Britain, with an ever-growing number of competent teachers to use them. But the bad news is that I have seen no improvement in the psychology of teaching. Take any random class of six students, and there are likely to be half a dozen different starting points on the learning curve. There is a vast difference in objectives and motivation between the competitively-minded teenager who aims to be a champion, and the elderly widow who wants to join the social bridge circle at her golf club. The latter will usually be quite content to remain a relatively unambitious player, so long as she can enjoy fun with her friends; the competitive youngster is certain to explore and experiment with all the gadgetry and tricks of the game. Therefore, the approach to teaching these two extremes needs to be markedly different.

Yet in all cases the first emphasis needs to be firmly on establishing confidence in handling the cards. Bidding methods used for reaching a final contract are usually developed naturally among the small individual groups who play together, whether they be two married couples after a jolly good dinner, or the members of the local tennis club. It really does not matter what bids are used to describe different types of hands (within reason!), provided that *both* the partner and the opponents understand the meaning. The essential factor is that declarer should develop the playing skills to make his contracts, before he bothers too much about how to bid them. This isn't a chicken-and-egg situation – playing the cards *is* more important than bidding them! Of course, bidding is important; but this is the area of the game which causes more dissent, frustration, turmoil, and – some would say – intrigue, than any other. Beginners and social players should be very sure of their ground before they start dabbling in the world of bidding systems. There are many players who spend their bridge lives in developing new systems – and modifying old ones (the Scientists). I commend the genuine pioneers, who made a valuable contribution to bidding theory; but I equally condemn the jerry-builders and cuckoos who do such harm to the common-sense understanding of basic bidding.

My maxims for good bidding are 'simplicity' and 'consistency', and for nearly thirty years now I've been using 'the power of the press' to preach the simple doctrine of the Acol system. The ideal of having a consensus throughout the length and breadth of Britain seems very desirable. It's nice to think that the Yorkshireman can partner the Cornishman on holiday, and, having agreed quickly to play *Daily Mail* Acol, they can spend time discussing signalling methods in defence!

TO MAKE A CAT LAUGH
by Jane Bodin

Jane Bodin
invites you to the

**WOLVERHAMPTON
BRIDGE
CLUB**

86 Tettenhall Rd., Wolverhampton WV1 4TF
Telephone 0902 20927

Benjamin, the resident cat at the Wolverhampton Bridge Club, was snoozing happily on the knee of one of his many admirers during a Thursday evening duplicate. This is a night when many of the keener players take part, so there is a good sprinkling of conventions and systems. Benji is named after 'Benjaminised Acol', which is Jane Bodin's (the club's proprietor) favourite bidding system. She reckons that his cheeky personality is akin to the Weak-Two opening bids of 2♡ and 2♠. These promise a 6-card suit and 5–10 points. They enable you to make your presence felt, even when the point count, like the cat, is quite small.

All of a sudden Benjamin pricked up his ears as the following hand came up:

```
         North           Dealer: South
         ♠ K 9 7 4 3     E/W Vul.
         ♡ A K 6 2
         ◇ 9 5 4
         ♣ 10
West                     East
♠ 6                      ♠ A
♡ 8 7 4                  ♡ Q J 9 5 3
◇ Q J 10 6 3             ◇ A 8 2
♣ A 6 3 2                ♣ K Q J 4
         South
         ♠ Q J 10 8 5 2
         ♡ 10
         ◇ K 7
         ♣ 9 8 7 5
```

South opened 2♠ (weak), West passed, and North came in with a blistering 4♠. What could East do? Vulnerable, with 17 points – he was powerless.

So 4♠ rolled home, even though the opponents have 24 points and fits in both minors. In fact, had East taken a gamble and bid, he would have got doubled as quick as a cat with a mouse and suffered a hefty penalty.

It's enough to make a cat laugh.

EAVESDROPPINGS

Aggrieved player to his lady partner: "Why did you not lead the suit I signalled for?"

Her unabashed reply: "I used my own judgement – I thought it the best!"
Diana Harrison

ELSPETH GETS IT WRONG
by Queenie Penguin

Over the years, the *Emperor Penguin* – the longest established club where the highest standard of play can be found in the whole of Antarctica – has slowly moved away from rubber bridge towards the more popular form of duplicate.

The success of duplicate has been due partly to the Master Point Scheme run by the Penguin Bridge Union, and partly to a very happy choice of club competitions on

the part of the *Emperor*'s Committee. Let me say first that duplicate is played every twenty-four hours at the *Emperor Penguin*, but it is on Tuesdays that the best players compete for various cups which – with the exception of the 'Iceberg Cup' – are all for individual competitions, one of the requirements being that members must play with at least ten different partners over a year. As a result, the club does not suffer from the cliquishness that affects other similar establishments at the South Pole: everybody plays with everybody else, particularly on non-Cup Nights (alternate Tuesdays) when the results do not count towards the official competitions.

It was on one such non-Cup Night that I visited the club and kibitzed Archibald Penguin and Elspeth. This was the first time Elspeth had been able to secure such an exalted Emperor for her partner, and she was understandably quite nervous. However, the evening had been very successful, Elspeth had slowly begun to relax, and Archibald's natural politeness had mellowed into a semblance of real friendliness. The last two rounds of the session unfortunately did not contribute to the happiness of the partnership.

South	*West*	*North*	*East*
1◇	NB	2♣	NB
2NT	NB	3◇	NB
3♠	NB	5◇	All Pass

Archibald
♠ K J 6
♡ J 7
◇ J 9 5 3
♣ K 8 6 2

Dealer: South
Love All

West
♠ 10 9 8 2
♡ A Q 6 4 2
◇ 10
♣ 10 7 3

East
♠ 5 4 3
♡ K 10 9 3
◇ Q 7 4 2
♣ 9 4

Elspeth
♠ A Q 7
♡ 8 5
◇ A K 8 6
♣ A Q J 5

As dealer, Elspeth contemplated her hand with suspicion. Playing with any of her regular cronies she would have opened with 2NT, but her heart holding might well incur Archibald's criticism, so she settled for 1◇. Over partner's 2♣, 2NT was forcing (15+ points, balanced), and 3♠ over Archibald's natural 3♢ could be taken as either a feature for no-trumps or the first move towards a slam. Archibald's firm 5♢ bid put a stop to any such ambitions.

West having led the ♠10, Elspeth surveyed dummy with mixed feelings. How wise she had been not to open 2NT – a 3NT contract would be doomed on the very predictable heart lead! And yet – how was she going to make 5♢? With two inescapable heart losers, it all came down to avoiding a loser in the trump suit. Missing both the Queen and the Ten, there wasn't a finesse position, so, having won the opening lead in hand, Elspeth played the ♢A hoping to find the ♢Q doubleton. West contributed the ♢10.

Now here was a problem. What was West's diamond holding, singleton Ten or Queen-Ten doubleton? After racking her brains in vain, Elspeth decided to carry on with her original plan, and bashed out the ♢K. When West showed out, it was all over, and declarer conceded one off.

As he entered the only minus 50 on a scoresheet full of 3NT by North-South, making with anything up to two overtricks, Archibald shook his head sadly. "South must always have opened 2NT," he said, "and West must have thought it unsafe to open the heart suit, thus leading a spade. Pity you did not make 5♢."

"I was on a guess," replied Elspeth, nettled. "I have no way of knowing what East's diamond holding is."

"It's not a matter of guessing," her distinguished partner retorted with some asperity. "It's a matter of probabilities. When the ♢10 comes down, there are still three diamonds out, and it is a statistical probability that East holds all of them."

'So, what it boils down to is that if an honour appears at round one, you finesse on round two,' thought Elspeth. 'We live and learn.'

Chalking down the bad result to experience, she moved to the next table and extracted her hand from another board.

The bidding was straightforward:

North	East	South	West
1♣	NB	1♡	1♠
2♡	NB	3♢	NB
4♡	All Pass		

Archibald   Dealer: North
♠ K 6 4 2   Game All
♡ K Q 10
♢ 6
♣ A K 9 7 5

West
♠ A 9 8 7 3
♡ 7 6 4 2
♢ K Q J 5
♣ —

East
♠ Q 10
♡ 5
♢ 10 9 8 3
♣ Q J 10 8 4 2

Elspeth
♠ J 5
♡ A J 9 8 3
♢ A 7 4 2
♣ 6 3

West led the ♢K, and Elspeth, once more, surveyed dummy with mixed feelings. There seemed to be twelve tricks for the taking, but the scarcity of communication between dummy and hand might well restrict the tally to ten – five hearts, two clubs, one diamond, one diamond ruff, and a spade if, as it seemed likely from the bidding, the Ace was right. Accurate timing seemed to be of the essence so, having won the opening lead with the ◇A, declarer led a spade. West went up with the Ace, dummy played low, and East contributed the ♠10 – a card which Elspeth viewed with some disfavour. This feeling intensified when West proceeded to lead the ♠3.

'Well,' thought Elspeth, 'now I know what to do,' and still thinking of the previous hand she played low from dummy. East won the ♠Q and returned a diamond, which was ruffed in dummy. Changing her plan of action, and now intending to cross-ruff the hand, declarer played the ♣A only to see it ruffed by West, who next led a trump. At this point, a thoroughly rattled Elspeth lost her head completely, and fluffed around to end one down in an eminently makeable contract.

Once more, Archibald entered the only minus on a traveller full of plus scores to North-South for 2♡, making with anything up to two overtricks. "You should not finesse the second spade," he pronounced, shaking his head even more sadly than before.

"But you said that if an honour appeared, the prob . . ."

"But this is a different situation altogether," Archibald interrupted. "From his partner's ♠10 West knows that you hold the ♠J, and he would never underlead the Queen to give you an extra trick."

'What this all amounts to,' thought Elspeth bitterly, ' is that there are no guidelines to be followed in this stupid game, and each hand poses a different problem. That's two in succession I've managed to get wrong. I'll never again be asked to play by a good player!'

But there she was, wrong again. Archibald's noble nature, and the 63% score which he knew they had achieved overall, made him take pity on the dejected, plump penguin who stood opposite him with tears in her eyes. Taking out his diary from the folds of shiny feathers, he said, not without gentleness: "Would you like another game? I'm afraid I'm booked on all Cup Nights, but some other time, perhaps . . .?"

A PSYCHIC PAUSE
by Bette Day

An earnest bridge player from Cowes
With a strong inclination to browse
His technique to enhance
Spent so long in a trance
He contacted his long-deceased spouse!"

THE *BRIDGE PLUS* QUIZ

Even if you are not a regular reader of BRIDGE PLUS, you may well be entertained by this quiz and the articles it refers to. Subscribers will have no problem in giving the right answers; non-subscribers can borrow back-numbers from their friends – but why not buy them, together with a subscription for the current year? *(Write to us at: Ryden Grange, Limecroft Road, Bisley, Surrey, GU21 2TH) (Solutions on page 51.)*

1. Who are the penguins portrayed on the right?
2. Who played a bridge match that lasted until 4 a.m. and was enlivened by endless drinks of vodka?
3. Which movement accompanied the recipe for *Crème Caramel* published in the 'Dinner and Bridge Series' (November 1990)?
4. How old was the youngest player at the 1990 World Championships?
5. Which bridge club has a resident cat called Benjamin?

6. Which entry in the 'Mr Bridge Dictionary' Series was illustrated by this cartoon?
7. Who advocated *A New Organization for Bridge Players* in the January 1991 'Soapbox'?
8. Which school ran a 24-hour Bridge Marathon in aid of the Romanian Orphanages?
9. Which convention was recommended by Madam Amanda to players born under the sign of Pisces?
10. Who wrote an article about cigarette cards?

11. Which article was illustrated by this cartoon?
12. Who took the *Kamikaze Finesse* in 'The Rubber Bridge Page' and allowed Mrs Harris to win her singleton ♣Q?
13. Who changed her partner, instead of changing her signalling system as advised by the Editor?
14. What, in Ron Pick's view, is *Better than Baked Beans*?
15. Who writes under the pseudonym of Queenie Penguin?

THERE'S NOWT SO QUEER AS FOLK

by Ron Pick and John Harper

The title of this article is particularly true at the bridge table, where two main personality traits emerge. Some people like to let things happen in a regular order, for tension to build up gradually until the final game is won. They may well feel that they like to play themselves in and not take too many chances early on in the game, and certainly to husband their best efforts until it really matters.

Others are busier by nature. As soon as they are in action they are firing on all cylinders and putting 100% effort into everything. The build-up to a climax is less important to them, since wherever they are is a crisis point. Each decision must be taken on its merits.

Given these two traits, then perhaps we can see why duplicate bridge grew out of rubber bridge. We suppose that the rubber bridge player expects a rubber of, say, five plus hands. He feels very cheated when he loses two straight games on the first two hands, and even slightly hard done by when he wins in the same manner. Understandably, he will pay less attention to a 1NT contract with seven certain tricks and a possible eighth trick. For the duplicate player (particularly for the pairs aficionado) all boards are the same in terms of importance. The only thing that matters is to outscore your opponents. Aggression pays, as does risk-taking.

The purpose of all this is to suggest that our two types of personalities are extremes. Most of us contain elements of both types, and may well enjoy both forms of bridge.

What then are the differences between the games in terms of laws? It is true that they are governed by different law books, the rubber game's laws dating back to 1981 whilst the duplicate game completely revised its laws in 1987. However, the first thing to say is that the differences are pretty minor. We will highlight these differences under five headings.

1. Preliminaries

Those who enter duplicate from rubber bridge are rendered uneasy by the lack of the ritual of cutting for partners, deal, choice of seats and of cards. All of this is spelled out in their code. When they get to a duplicate evening they may well find that their position is determined by a random draw, or by something like 'first come, first served' which do not appear to obey any organisational rules. What they will be told is when and where to move, and that they may not change positions after they have started. They will feel, too, that the preliminaries in which anyone takes a board, shuffles, deals, and puts the cards back in the boards regardless of dealer is all a bit casual. Our only comment here is that we should remember, when testing the water, that the preliminaries represent the first touch of a toe at the surface, and we would expect you to notice the difference.

2. Dealing with Irregularities

Here the laws are very similar indeed. Duplicate players are thoroughly spoilt by having their friendly Tournament Director present and ever willing to sort out their problems. In rubber bridge there may be fewer problems, but when they do occur players normally have to apply the laws themselves. The principles about noting the fact that an irregularity has occurred are identical. Errors corrected by the players themselves by agreement *must* be accepted at rubber bridge, but only *may* be accepted at duplicate. The law concerning the right to penalise if the non-offending side takes premature action is identical.

We can only admire the ingenuity of the duplicate law makers who arranged that many laws (e.g. those concerning unauthorised information) bear the same numbers in both codes. In effect, where the unauthorised information comes from partner, the laws are consistent; where the unauthorised information is extraneous, the rubber bridge laws are silent, since in a normal situation the possibility is remote.

3. The Auction

Now we come into another area where differences do appear. The habits of *Alerting* partner's conventional bids and saying *Stop* or *Skip* before a jump-bid are peculiar to duplicate. These rituals are fairly easy to learn and, in fact, help the smooth running of the game. Also the player new to duplicate bridge must learn to fill in a convention card, though many rubber bridge players manage very well with "What do you play?" – "Strong No-trump, Stayman and Blackwood."

Changes of calls after incorrect explanations are covered by the laws of duplicate, and provisions are made for the director to adjudicate an adjusted score if the non-offending side has been damaged. The problem never comes up at rubber bridge, as generally people are not allowed to use complicated systems and conventions. If someone gives a wrong explanation it is usually because there is no partnership agreement, and consequently no penalty applies. Only when both partnerships have allowed each other to play conventions would the laws of rubber, at the discretion of the club's director, be superseded by those applying to duplicate bridge.

4. The Play

The *face down* opening lead is another peculiarity of the duplicate game although, as with alerting and stop bids, it is something that helps the game along. The power of a declarer to become dummy when a defender makes an opening lead out of turn is not given in rubber bridge. There it is a matter of propriety *not* to spread a hand deliberately to achieve this objective.

Also, the duplicate declarer is protected by the laws from his excesses when he decides to lead from the wrong hand. As with his rubber bridge counterpart, the defenders have the option either to accept or reject the lead. However, when the lead is rejected, the duplicate declarer is merely told to lead from the correct hand – whereas his rubber bridge counterpart must, if possible, lead a card of the same suit as his mistaken lead. This is obviously a severe penalty when declarer was intending to take a finesse. Should he ignore this instruction, he is deemed to have revoked!

Dummy has, however, greater rights in rubber bridge, since there he may question any player about a possible revoke. In both sets of laws he is banned from drawing attention to an irregularity during play – although he may try to prevent one occurring. There is a minor difference between the codes in the above cases. Dummy (at duplicate) may try to prevent *his partner* from doing something wrong, whereas at rubber bridge he may try to prevent *any player* from committing an irregularity. In both codes dummy's rights are virtually eliminated if, "on his own initiative", he see another player's cards.

Probably the greatest difference in the laws concerning play comes in the section on revokes. Here the law at rubber bridge follows the pre-1987 pattern of considering which side took the trick in order to decide whether the penalty should be one or two tricks. At duplicate the matter is much more complicated, involving which player of the offending side won the trick, which card was played to the revoke trick, and that card's ability to take a later trick before determining the size of the penalty. Certainly this is one of those cases where, at duplicate, the director must be called.

It is necessary to mention the law concerning the agreement of number of tricks in the duplicate game, since this is an area where mistakes can occur easily. At rubber, obviously, it is much more difficult to appropriate a trick unless you forcibly wrest it out of the opponents' hands!

Hey

Claims and concessions, if disputed, diverge in their treatment. At duplicate, play ceases, and it is up to the Tournament Director to rule on the basis of the stated claim or concession and the cards remaining at the time of the claim. At rubber, the play continues with the claimant's hand faced, so that the players test the validity of the claim. The same yardsticks are used in both games.

5. Scoring

At duplicate bridge, scoring is artificial, in that – starting with the same computation for tricks or undertricks made – the results are then processed firstly through the addition of bonuses on each hand for successful part-scores, games, or slams. Each hand is a single unit of the game, and the result on it does not affect the succeeding hand. Secondly, the scores are further processed, either by match-pointing (at pairs) or by conversion to IMPs (at teams), except at aggregate or point-a-board scoring.

At rubber bridge, the bonuses – on a hand-to-hand basis – are confined to slams and honours (the latter are unknown to the duplicate player). It is only when the final game is won that game bonuses appear. The only processing to be done now is to calculate the net score of each pair.

There are, too, differences in the scoring of doubled contracts in the two games. Before 1987 the rules were identical: a doubled contract made was awarded '50 for the insult'. In 1987 the duplicate law introduced a bonus of 100 points for redoubled contracts, whereas at rubber this remained 50. Non-vulnerable, doubled undertricks are more expensive at duplicate (where they cost 100 points for the first, 200 for the second and third, but 300 each from the fourth onwards, whereas at rubber the first is worth 100 and all subsequent undertricks are penalized at 200 points apiece). Thus, at duplicate, it is harder to sacrifice against opponents' slam contracts.

✶✶✶✶✶

From the contrasts outlined above you will note that whilst the games may be different in appearance, the actual playing is identical, and the results of errors of procedure are the same or very similar. We hope that duplicate players may decide to turn up for the odd rubber, and the rubber bridge player will invest the odd session in trying the fun of duplicate.

Bridge Plus Poems
BRIDGE OVER THE WATER
by Lucy Murray

'Two countries separated by the same language' (George Bernard Shaw)

For two long years once did I grapple
With bridge as played in the 'Big Apple'.
They seemed to like the way I spoke
As one New Yorker (for a joke)
Said: "Honey, you're a limey kid,
"I love to hear you say 'No Bid!'!"
Where I said 'Stop' in British style
Their version was more versatile:
"I'm just about to make a skip,
"Please wait ten seconds, pip by pip."

In New York you booked a table
As North/South, you then were able
To smoke or, if you felt that way,
To keep the dreaded weed at bay.
One day my partner, quite a joker –
English, and a heavy smoker –
Was asked by an approaching dame
As she sat down to play the game:
"Say, does my ciggie give you yips?"
(One was protruding from her lips.)

"Madam," said my partner Paul,
"Get it clear for good and all,
"Smoking is, if you are able,
"Compulsory when at my table!"
She bowed her neatly coiffured head;
"Oh, gee, I'm mortified," she said
"I didn't know you banned the snout!"
And hastily she stubbed it out!

A NIGHTMARE OF A HAND

by Julianna Lees

Life at Keddington Grange is never dull. Between running *I'm Potty Over Bridge* by mail order and nipping over to our property in the Dordogne four or five times a year, we still manage the occasional houseparty for bridge lovers.

It's hard enough to find a date to get four dinner guests together, let alone four strangers for several days, who need to be reasonably compatible – socially as well as regards standard of play – so I prefer to take groups of three or four friends who have agreed a date already. Our first group this summer consisted of four young wives from Harrogate, all civil servants working together, *(pictured opposite)* who ditched husbands and children for a good weekend of country living and non-stop bridge. We had a whale of a time, playing in swimsuits by the pool, two tables with local friends on Saturday night, and stupefied after a huge Sunday roast. The quartet left heavier, wiser, and very relaxed, and asked to return with four more colleagues!

The next group was more concerned to maintain their waistlines, so salads and fruit were very high on the menu, and the rarefied diet contributed towards fiercer competition. This party comprised two charming ladies from Gloucestershire, plus one very lively octogenarian mum and a lively headmistress from Oxfordshire, previously unknown to the others, but soon the centre of the group. They opted for a mid-week stay, so we were able to go to the Club for an evening of duplicate – a baptism of fire for the two friends who survived the experience with flying colours.

This group also enjoyed an evening of Chicago with the local talent, in the course of which I picked up the South hand shown below.

Naturally, I opened 2♣ and partner, who must have been napping, responded a negative 2◇. Over my 2♠ rebid, partner offered 2NT so, having received two negative bids, I concluded the auction with 4♠ and nearly had a fit when North's dummy hand went down.

"Betty!" I cried in dismay. "We should be in a slam!" I spoke too soon. This is what happened.

North
♠ 10 5
♡ J 10 3 2
◇ K Q 5 4
♣ J 7 3

South
♠ A K J 4 3
♡ A K 8 5
◇ A 6
♣ K 2

Virginia (West) led a small diamond. I played small from dummy, Olive (East) contributed the ◇10, and I popped my Ace on it. I then returned the opposition's lead, intending to void myself of diamonds, get onto the table, and attempt the spade finesse. It was unlikely, considering my diamond shortage, that West had led from a singleton.

This, however, was exactly what had happened. A small trump took the trick and back came a heart. With a feeling of foreboding I played the ♡10 from dummy and, sure enough, Olive ruffed! The full deal was as shown.

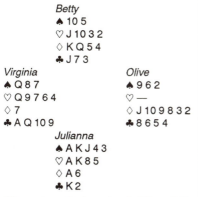

Betty
♠ 10 5
♡ J 10 3 2
◇ K Q 5 4
♣ J 7 3

Virginia
♠ Q 8 7
♡ Q 9 7 6 4
◇ 7
♣ A Q 10 9

Olive
♠ 9 6 2
♡ —
◇ J 10 9 8 3 2
♣ 8 6 5 4

Julianna
♠ A K J 4 3
♡ A K 8 5
◇ A 6
♣ K 2

The rest can be imagined. Olive, following some infernal instinct, led a club through my King. Virginia took this with her Ace, cashed the ♣Q, and led another heart for Olive to ruff. By this time the opposition had won five tricks and I was down two. There was, however, more to come: East now played a diamond which I ruffed with the ♠J – West overruffing with the ♠Q (so much for my intended finesse!) and returning a third heart which East ruffed with glee. When she returned a diamond, I had had enough: I ruffed with the ♠A, drew the last trump, and just about managed to win the rest of the tricks. Nevertheless, the result was still four down.

Could you have done better? My mother still says *she* would, but it's always easy after the event, isn't it?

AN EARLY TURKISH BATH
by Eddie Horsup

Turks love to play backgammon in cafés. When I lived in Istanbul some years ago I went with some friends to one, and we decided instead to play bridge. I picked up dismal cards, with only the odd glass of raki to console me. What proved the final hand of the evening was typical of its predecessors.

The dealer, an American fellow-teacher named John, opened 3♣ on my right. I passed mechanically, as did my student Erim on my left. My partner Savash bid 3NT and with a feeling of gloom I converted to 4♠. This was the hand that was reconstructed from memory somewhat later.

The ♣10 was led, and the smirk trying to break out on Erim's face caused me unease. I played guessing games. A 3♣ opening should show a 7-card suit, but John was that untrustworthy sort of opponent who might bid on six cards. If there were seven clubs in his hand, I would win with the Ace, draw trumps, and run off winners. If, however,

```
                 Savash
                 ♠ J 8 7 3
                 ♡ A K J 4
                 ◇ A K
                 ♣ A 7 2
    Erim                      John
 ♠ A K 10                   ♠ —
 ♡ Q 10 8 6                 ♡ 9 5 3
 ◇ 8 7 6 4                  ◇ Q 10 9 3
 ♣ 10 3                     ♣ K Q J 9 8 6
                 Me
                 ♠ Q 9 6 5 4 2
                 ♡ 7 2
                 ◇ J 5 2
                 ♣ 5 4
```

John had opened with only six, Erim would have a second club to lead when in with the ♠A, and a third club could mean a trump promotion.

While I was pondering my action, a burly chap swaggered over and made some sneering remark in Turkish. He looked at me and gestured under his chin to indicate my beard. I was evidently being insulted, and Savash took exception. He got up and replied vehemently. There were more jibes from the stranger, and Erim and Savash became embroiled in a slanging match. John and I, neither with such mastery of Turkish, looked on uncertainly.

I retained my cards in my hand, the other kept firmly on the table. This was the first hand I had played all evening, and I was not going to give in easily. Despite my efforts, the card table was hurled across the room, and the hand lost. Chairs were raised and used on anyone within range, just as in a bar brawl in Westerns. When someone I did not know, full of apologies for everything, ushered me downstairs, it seemed a good time to go. I went back to my flat and took an earlier bath than expected.

When I met Erim the next day we had each recovered our composure, and he assured me that the trump promotion would have defeated the contract. "Not so," I countered. "Two rounds of hearts and a heart ruff would have put me on lead, and I would have led through your trump holding. Then when you lead a second club I can ruff the third with the ♠Q."

"Ah, yes," was Erim's reply, "but do you make this play if that man is not come?"

* * * * *

There is nothing fictional about this story. That's the way it was, though time may have dimmed the memory of some of the spot cards. I would love to play again in Istanbul. I am sure that with bearded foreigners now ten a penny, it could not happen again.

People and Bridge

MEMOIRS OF A NOVICE: THREE NO-TRUMPS OR BUST
by Sue Lowe

Rita plays bridge five times a week; she plays for fun and is unambitious. She is an easy person to partner, and prefers 3NT with three overtricks to bidding a slam.

I tell her before we start that I have this phobia of playing in no-trumps. "Right," she says, "tonight's the night!" On the first hand we play I open a weak one no-trump. Rita passes and grins, her eyes sparkling: "Well, partner, I've nine points, so you can make it." We do, with an overtrick. "Just luck," I say.

Two hands later I open a heart, she replies with a spade. I hold four good clubs and three diamonds. Here we go again: she immediately raises my one no-trump to three. Get rid of your losers, I remind myself; set up the long suit and make sure to be able to cross from one hand to the other.

That evening I play in no-trumps eight times, and it gradually becomes easier. 'Play five times a week,' I think to myself, 'and I'll be able to do it in my sleep.' I actually do dream of bridge!

There is a pair at the club who withhold their Aces time and again. I'm developing a system which pays dividends. I take all the tricks I need in that suit, and then laugh inwardly as, on the final boss ◇2, the ♣A and ♠A are discarded.

I'm not afraid of no-trump contracts anymore!

FAIR ENOUGH

by P.F. Saunders

"I'm not going to bother you after all," announced my granddaughter.

"Good. What about?"

"This – from last night's rubber bridge. I meant to ask you to settle a bet, but I've just managed to solve the problem myself."

"Is that a diagram? Let me see if I can spot what the problem was without you telling me."

West	North	East	South
1♠	Dbl	NB	1NT
NB	3NT	All Pass	

I studied the diagram.

"I believe," I said slowly, "that you were North, and Bruce South; that West led the ♠8; that South went one down; that I know why; that he blamed your second bid; that you blamed his play; that one of you (you, I fancy) made the inevitable bet; and that I was supposed to decide who won."

"You're exactly right! How do you do it?"

North — Dealer: West — Game All
- ♠ 7 4
- ♡ A 8 6 4
- ◇ A K 10 2
- ♣ A K 7

West
- ♠ A K J 8 5
- ♡ J 9 5 3
- ◇ Q
- ♣ Q 10 6

East
- ♠ 9 2
- ♡ 10 7
- ◇ J 9 5 3
- ♣ 8 5 4 3 2

South
- ♠ Q 10 6 3
- ♡ K Q 2
- ◇ 8 7 6 4
- ♣ J 9

"At my age, you mean? It *is* rather remarkable. My only difficulty was telling which of you was which. I put you in the North seat because you are the more optimistic bidder, and the rest was easy. After the standard opening lead, the average declarer ... do you mind, either of you, being an average declarer?"

"It's a compliment."

"The average declarer wins, leads a diamond, is startled by the appearance of the Queen, wins again, sees various chances of nine tricks, cannot resist first trying another high diamond in the hope of dropping the Jack, and is disappointed."

"You're right again. Bruce next tried the hearts, and they did not break, so he turned to the clubs, playing Ace, King, and another. Unfortunately, West saw what was happening and unblocked, so the third club went to East, and that was that. *But* I've been thinking. All Bruce had to do was throw West in with the fourth heart instead of playing on clubs. Now West has to give him a spade trick or lead away from the ♣Q. There's your ninth trick."

"Very neat. There is only one trouble, I think. West may not lead *away* from the Queen, he may lead the Queen itself."

42

"What difference does that make?"

"It blocks the suit."

"Good heavens, so it does. There is no entry to dummy now. There goes my money."

"What exactly was the bet?"

"I bet Bruce that he could have made the contract."

"Oh, I daresay you might win that all right. Suppose he doesn't play a second high diamond at trick three, but tries the hearts first. East shows out, and South can count West for five spades, four hearts, and therefore four minor suit cards – one of which is the ◇Q and another, he hopes, the ♣Q. So he does just what you suggest – throws West in with the fourth heart. Let's look at the position after six tricks:

"Yes, you win your bet. West is on lead and can make two spade tricks but, no matter how he plays after that, he is bound to give South four of the remainder and his contract. There is no longer any point in West leading the ♣Q, because dummy still has a diamond entry. By the way, if it turns out that after all West has the ◇J instead of a club, the diamonds break and South gets an overtrick."

```
              ♠ 7
              ♡ —
              ◇ A 10 2
              ♣ A K 7
♠ A K J 5                 ♠ 2
♡ —                       ♡ —
◇ —                       ◇ J 9 5
♣ Q 10 6                  ♣ 8 5 4
              ♠ Q 6 3
              ♡ —
              ◇ 8 7
              ♣ J 9
```

"Beautiful. I'd never have spotted all that. I'm beginning to think I'll have trouble in making Bruce pay up! Perhaps I ought to call the bet off."

"Now that you've dragged me into it, why not let me decide for you?"

"I'm rather suspicious of you now – you look mischievous. All right, you decide."

"Bruce played the hand wrongly, and was also wrong, in my opinion, in criticising your bid – you had every right to expect him to hold rather more than just a spade guard. On the other hand, you didn't really know how he could have made it, or even that he went wrong at trick three. We only got at it ourselves by seeing all the cards. I think you both lose. I hope the bet was a large one."

"Why, if nobody wins? Actually, it was 50p."

I found the right coin, dropped it in the R.S.P.C.A. box which was at hand, and pronounced sentence. "You both owe me 25p," I said.

P.F. Saunders and his granddaughter

<table>
<tr><td>

David Parry writes for

Telephone 071-822 2002

</td><td>

REQUIREMENTS FOR AN ACOL TWO
by David Parry

The tournament player, increasingly concerned with disrupting the bidding of the opponents, is often prepared to sacrifice the constructive use of some 2-level bids in order to incorporate a

</td></tr>
</table>

range of pre-emptive gadgets. However, most rubber bridge players retain the traditional Acol approach where 2♣ is the strongest call, whilst other 2-level openers show powerful hands based on length in the suit opened.

The exact requirements for an Acol Two have never been easily defined. For the beginner, a simple rule is 20–22 points and a 6-card suit. Another definition is in terms of playing tricks: the number of tricks which you are likely to take if your long suit is trumps. Some texts suggest a minimum of eight playing tricks, but eight-and-a-half is probably a better benchmark.

If you decide to adopt the playing-trick criterion, be careful not to confuse pre-emptive 4-level openers, especially vulnerable 4-level openers, with Strong Twos. Both are likely to have eight-plus tricks, but the 4-level opener will be based on a 7 or 8-card suit with little or no defensive strength, whilst the 2-level bid typically shows a 6-carder with outside values.

Another question is whether a Strong Two can be bid on a 5-card suit. Rarely, would be my answer, but occasionally a hand with two well-stuffed 5-card (or longer) suits might qualify.

Another way to consider the matter is to ask yourself two questions: firstly, whether if partner passes a 1-level opener there is a serious risk of missing game, and secondly whether after a 1-level opening bid you would be unable to describe the full power of your hand. If the answer to either question is yes, then a 2-level bid is usually in order. What would you open on the following hands?

Hand (a)	Hand (b)	Hand (c)	Hand (d)	Hand (e)
♠ A K Q J 7 6	♠ A K Q 9 7 6 4 3	♠ A Q 9 7	♠ A K J 8 7	♠ A K J 10 6
♡ A K J 10	♡ Q J 10	♡ A K 5	♡ A 6	♡ K Q J 10 6
◊ 5	◊ —	◊ A Q J 7 6	◊ A Q 4	◊ A 5
♣ 3 2	♣ 3 2	♣ 3	♣ Q J 7	♣ 2

With *Hand (a)*, open 2♠. You have nine plus playing tricks, could well make game if partner held four small spades and nothing else, and would have great difficulty showing the full strength of your hand after a 1♠ opener. Holding *Hand (b)*, an opening bid of 4♠ is recommended. Once again, you have nine tricks – but virtually no defensive strength.

On *Hand (c)*, the best bid is 1◇. It is difficult to assess precisely the playing strength of this hand. My estimate would be about seven-and-a-half tricks.

Holding *Hand (d)*, open 2NT. With balanced hands, the point count provides a very accurate method of valuation, and there is no need to count playing tricks. Conversely, on *Hand (e)*, you must open 2♠. With nine-plus tricks and two well-packed 5-carders, this is a good example of a 2-level opener without a 6-card suit. Again you might well miss a game and could not hope to describe the full potential of your hand after a 1-level opening bid.

The following hand is more difficult. With East-West vulnerable, dealer North, what would you suggest North opens?

North
♠ A J 5
♡ A K
◇ A K 8 6 4 2
♣ 6 4

South
♠ Q 8 3
♡ 8 7 4
◇ J
♣ A J 10 9 8 2

An argument could be made for one or two diamonds, or perhaps 2NT. None is ideal, but with so many Aces and Kings my vote goes to 2◇.

South is not quite worth a positive response. The standard negative reply is 2NT, but a better system is to play *Herbert Negatives*, where the cheapest bid – here 2♡ – becomes the negative response, and 2NT replaces the lost positive – here in hearts. Over 2♡ North can rebid 2NT to suggest a semi-balanced hand.

Whatever the auction, the final contract is likely to be 3NT. How would you plan the play from the South seat on the lead of the ♡Q?

You have six top tricks and could develop others in clubs or diamonds. On the face of it, you need either a 3–3 break in diamonds (36%) or a 3–2 club break (68%) and the double club finesse (75%), apparently a 51% chance. The problem with tackling the clubs is that you have no sure outside entry to South's hand, and if the opponents duck the first round or East plays an honour, you will not be able to enjoy the suit. At the table, South decided to try the diamonds instead. He played Ace, King, and another, but when the suit broke 4–2 he eventually had to concede defeat. However, he missed a chance. Did you spot it?

Right, you should play a low diamond to the Jack initially. As you can see from the full deal opposite, this gives you the extra chance of developing the suit if either opponent started with 10-9 doubleton.

North
♠ A J 5
♡ A K
◇ A K 8 6 4 2
♣ 6 4

West
♠ 7 6 2
♡ Q J 10 9 6
◇ 10 9
♣ Q 5 3

East
♠ K 10 9 4
♡ 5 3 2
◇ Q 7 5 3
♣ K 7

South
♠ Q 8 3
♡ 8 7 4
◇ J
♣ A J 10 9 8 2

DISTAFF TRANSFERS

by Malcolm Simpson

I've just invented a new bidding system. Before I elaborate further, let me demonstrate the shortcomings of the Acol System with a couple of example hands.

Hand (a)	The bidding:		Hand (b)	The bidding:	
♠ K J 5 3 2	*Wife*	*Husband*	♠ K 7 6 2	*Wife*	*Husband*
♡ A 7 4	1NT	3♠	♡ K 5	1♠	?
◇ K Q 2	3NT	?	◇ A 7 5 2		
♣ J 8			♣ K J 5		

What do you bid next?

Any self-respecting husband will know that on *Hand (a)* the obvious bid is 4♠ – because even with a 5–2 fit, you are more likely to make the contract than she is, excluding the fact that she is stubborn enough to bid 3NT with a 3-card fit anyway.

With *Hand (b)*, the money bid has to be 3NT. You only have to make nine tricks. If *you* cannot, how on earth do you expect *her* to make ten? Any exploratory bid risks a no-trump rebid from partner, leaving you no sensible resting place.

So the Acol System is hopelessly inadequate for husband-wife pairs, where the partnership is handicapped because the bidding strategy assumes that the wife will play as many contracts as her better half. This fatal assumption often forces the husband into inferior contracts in an attempt to restore the balance. My solution is for the wife to adopt a Tranfers System, while the husband sticks to natural bids. How does this work?

In the case of opening bids, it is imperative for the wife to avoid opening with a 5-card major, or in no-trumps. This enables us to lay down a completely new set of opening bids for the female partner:

> 1♣ = 13–19, unsuitable for any other 1-level bid.
> 1◇ = 13–19, 5 hearts.
> 1♡ = 13–19, 5 spades.
> 1♠ = 12–14 balanced, or Acol Two in a minor.

(I regard this bid as a stroke of genius. When hubby makes his response, the stronger hand type is shown by jumping in the *opposite* minor.)

> 2♣ = 23+ points.
> 2◇ = Acol Two in hearts.
> 2♡ = Acol Two in spades.
> 2♠ = 20–22 balanced.

> 3♣/◇/♡/♠ = Pre-emptive bid in the next suit up.
> 1NT/2NT/3NT = Definitely not allowed.

The husband, of course, follows normal Acol principles.

I do appreciate that the current E.B.U. directives prohibit a partnership playing two different systems, but this is a very shortsighted doctrine. I am sure that this bit of dictatorial legislation can be overcome with effective lobbying from those sympathetic to my cause.

As you will appreciate, it would take many pages to describe the complete system (maybe there is scope for a new book here). Let me whet your appetite with a couple of sequences.

Wife	Husband
♠ K 7 5 2	♠ A 9 8
♡ A 5 3	♡ K J 7 6
◇ Q 10 4	◇ K 8 5
♣ Q J 8	♣ K 3 2

Wife	Husband
1♠ (a)	2♣ (b)
2♡ (c)	3NT (d)

(a) 12–14 balanced or Acol Two in a minor.

(b) Stayman.

(c) Opposite major. We can't let her bid hearts with hearts, in case there is a fit. If a spade fit is discovered, then we are forced to play in no-trumps. Not the ideal contract, but no system is perfect. We do, however, allow some freedom of choice. The opening bidder is allowed to correct to 4♠ with a singleton. Admittedly this is not a common occurrence as it is not compatible with a legal opening bid.

(d) To play.

Wife	Husband
♠ A 3 2	♠ K 8 7 4
♡ 3	♡ A 7 5 2
◇ A K Q 6 5 2	◇ J 4
♣ A K 5	♣ Q 7 2

Wife	Husband
1♠ (a)	1NT (b)
3♣ (c)	3◇ (d)
4NT (e)	5◇ (f)
5NT (g)	6◇ (h)
NB (j)	

(a) 12–14 balanced or Acol Two in a minor.

(b) Hogging the contract and signing off over 12–14 balanced.

(c) Acol Two in diamonds.

(d) Hogging the contract in diamonds and slam interest.

(e)/(f)/(g)/(h) Blackwood.

(j) Or 6NT in match-pointed pairs. Note that the declaration is still in the correct hand.

See you all at the next mixed pairs!

ARE YOU A GOOD DEFENDER?

by Morag Malcolm

Most players like to play the contract, and not so many like to defend. Yet it is just as important for defenders as for declarer to listen to the bidding, to try to place the high cards, and to plan the best line.

North
♠ A K J 9 4
♡ 7 6 3
♢ —
♣ Q J 10 9 5

EXAMPLE 1

West reaches 4♡ and North plays Ace, King and another spade.

South ruffs the third spade, and now what? North could have played any one of his three remaining spades, but he chose the Jack. By playing his highest remaining spade, he is asking his partner to return a diamond (the higher of the remaining suits). South does this, and his partner ruffs to set the contract.

West
♠ 8 6 2
♡ A Q J 10 4
♢ 8 4 3
♣ A K

Dummy
♠ Q 7 5
♡ K 9 8
♢ A K Q 10 2
♣ 4 3

South
♠ 10 3
♡ 5 2
♢ J 9 7 6 5
♣ 8 7 6 2

EXAMPLE 2

East plays in 4♡. South leads the ♠K. The ♠3 is played from dummy. As North, what are you going to do, and why?

North can see two spade tricks and the ♣A. To defeat this contract, another trick is needed – so North encourages with the ♠8, wins the second spade with the Ace and switches to the ♢6. East has no chance now, unless North has the ♢K, so he finesses and loses four tricks (two spades, one diamond and one club).

North
♠ A 8 5 4
♡ 9 7 2
♢ J 8 7 6
♣ A 5

Dummy
♠ 7 3
♡ K J 8 6
♢ 4 2
♣ K Q J 10 6

EXAMPLE 3

East is in 4♡. South leads the ♢J. North wins with the ♢A and continues with the ♢K. Which card should you play as South?

North must have a doubleton (else he would have played his diamond honours in different order), so you must show him your entry by playing the ♢10. This shows

48

North
♠ 9 8 7 3 2
♡ 7 5 2
◇ A K
♣ 10 9 7

South
♠ A 4
♡ 8
◇ J 10 8 4 3
♣ J 6 5 3 2

the higher suit (excluding trumps). Now North returns a spade and you defeat the contract by giving him his diamond ruff. The East-West hands are as below.

Notice that even if West is the declarer in 4♡, the contract should still be defeated. North leads the ◇K, then the ◇A (reverse of normal play), so South plays the ◇J at trick two again, to show the spade entry.

Dummy
♠ Q J 5
♡ A 9 6
◇ Q 7 5
♣ K Q 8 4

East
♠ K 10 6
♡ K Q J 10 4 3
◇ 9 6 2
♣ A

EXAMPLE 4

The contract is 4♡ by West. Should it make on the lead of the ♣A?

The answer is no – not if North and South signal correctly.

South plays the ♣Q at trick one. This says that South has *either* the singleton Queen *or* both Queen and Jack, in other words it tells North that if he plays a second club South can win it. North plays the ◇3 and, after one round of hearts, North is on lead again. He plays his lowest club to his partner's Jack and now he gets a diamond ruff to defeat the contract.

North
♠ Q 10 5 2
♡ A 7 6
◇ 3
♣ A K 8 4 2

West
♠ 8 3
♡ K Q 10 8 3
◇ 10 7 5 4
♣ 10 5

Dummy
♠ A K J
♡ J 9 5 2
◇ A K Q J
♣ 6 3

South
♠ 9 7 6 4
♡ 4
◇ 9 8 6 2
♣ Q J 9 7

EXAMPLE 5

North
♠ 4 3
♡ Q 7 2
◇ 8 7 6 5 2
♣ 10 9 8

East	South	West	North
1◇	1♡	1♠	NB
3♠	NB	4♠	All Pass

West
♠ K Q J 10 7
♡ 9 4 3
◇ J 4
♣ Q J 7

Dummy
♠ A 8 6 2
♡ 10 5
◇ K Q 10 9 3
♣ A K

South
♠ 9 5
♡ A K J 8 6
◇ A
♣ 6 5 4 3 2

North leads the ♡2. West appears to have only three losers (two hearts and one diamond). South wins trick one with the ♡K, cashes the ◇A, and returns the ♡8 (a McKenney signal) to his partner's Queen. North gives his partner a diamond ruff, and 4♠ goes one down. How did South know that his partner had the ♡Q?

49

Normally you lead low from an honour and South can see all other honours, so his only chance is to play North for the ♡Q. North knows that his partner wants a diamond ruff, as he can see East's strong diamonds – it would be silly for South to play as he did without a singleton Ace.

EXAMPLE 6

North	East	South	West
1♢	3♠	4♡	All Pass

Dummy
♠ Q 8
♡ 9 8 3
♢ A Q J 4 2
♣ A Q 6

West
♠ 6 2
♡ K 10 2
♢ 6 5
♣ K 9 7 5 3 2

East
♠ A K 9 7 5 4 3
♡ 4
♢ 9 7
♣ 10 8 4

South
♠ J 10
♡ A Q J 7 6 5
♢ K 10 8 3
♣ J

West leads the ♠6. East wins with the King and plays a second round of spades – everybody following. What next? A diamond or a club look bad for the defence, so East tries to promote a trump trick for his partner. He returns the ♠3. South plays the ♡J, and what does West do?

Too often, West grabs this trick and the defence is now over – 4♡ making ten tricks. West should pause and think. If he refuses to overruff, he will have the ♡K-10-2 over South's A-Q-7-6-5. He must now make two trump tricks, and this defeats 4♡.

EXAMPLE 7

West plays in 4♠ and North leads the ♡10. The contract looks rock solid, with only one spade and two hearts to lose – but South plays three rounds of hearts, West ruffing with the ♠J. West enters dummy with a club and leads a spade. South wins, and plays a fourth round of hearts. As the cards lie, North's ♠10 is promoted.

Again, South took his only chance (a slim one, maybe) and it succeeded.

North
♠ 10 6 5
♡ 10 3
♢ 8 3 2
♣ J 9 8 6 3

West
♠ K Q J 8 7 4
♡ 8 6
♢ K
♣ K Q 7 4

Dummy
♠ 9 3 2
♡ J 4 2
♢ A Q J 10 6 5
♣ A

South
♠ A
♡ A K Q 9 7 5
♢ 9 7 4
♣ 10 5 2

EXAMPLE 8

North plays in 3NT and East leads the ♣5. North can count eight tricks on the lead, and should try to steal another club quickly. East must be alert and take this with his Ace. West must be careful to signal properly, so that his partner will switch to the correct suit. West must discourage spades and diamonds, but he must hold on to four hearts – as a heart switch by East will defeat 3NT. Too often, players are so keen to tell partner what to play that they throw away tricks. Note that a heart discard by West lets the contract home.

North
♠ A J
♡ 9 7 3
◇ A 8 4 3
♣ K Q 7 6

West
♠ 9 8 5 3 2
♡ A K J 10
◇ 10 9 7 2
♣ —

East
♠ 7 6 4
♡ 8 4 2
◇ 6 5
♣ A 9 8 5 4

Dummy
♠ K Q 10
♡ Q 6 5
◇ K Q J
♣ J 10 3 2

*****

Your defence will improve if you think about the bidding, your leads, and your partner's signals. Make sure both of you are on the same wavelength and trust each other's cards and not the opposition. If you would like to read more, then *Guide to Better Acol Bridge* by Ron Klinger is a super book for improving your own play and defence.

Morag Malcolm

THE BRIDGE PLUS QUIZ – SOLUTIONS TO PAGE 33

1. Macaroni, Archibald, and the Jackass (from: *A Matter of Style*, in the 'Bridge at the South Pole' series, March 1991); 2. Peter Stocken and his Russian guests (*Vodka and Bridge*, October 1990); 3. The 'Roving Dummy' Movement, described by Ron Heath; 4. Ten. It was Godefroy de Tessières, playing in a family team comprising his father Jean-Bernard, his sister Stéphanie (18), and his three brothers Thibault (14), Aymeric (15) and Cristophe (21) (November 1990); 5. Wolverhampton.(*Bridge Club of the Month*, December 1990); 6. *P for . . . Phantom Pair* (May 1991); 7. Alan Caves of Milton Keynes; 8. St. George's (as reported in 'Bridge Around the Country' in January 1991; 9. Appropriately – DABS! (March 1991); 10. Keith Jarrett (*Try the Vanderbilt Club with 'Slam'*, April 1991); 11. *The Threat of the Ten*, an article in the 'Improve Your Defence ' series by Eric Crowhurst (July 1991); 12. It was the author, Malcolm Simpson. This was the only time the male player in the Ladies' Circle admitted to doing anything silly! (April 1991); 13. Diane Berber (*Letters to the Editor*, May 1991); 14. Bidding Boxes. Ron Pick summarized the laws concerning bidding boxes in his 'Tournament Player' series in July 1991; 15. I won't tell you!

PLAY IT AGAIN, SAM!

by Peter Rowlett

What makes a good card-player – specifically, a good dummy player? You'd expect an individual's skill at what is essentially an exercise in logic, judgment, and memory, to correspond to that which he displays in other spheres of activity – his profession, perhaps. When we put our partner the doctor into 3NT and watch him go two off through faulty diagnosis, do we quietly switch to another practice? When our partner the solicitor mangles a contract, are we reluctant to put our house conveyancing his way? I don't think so. Look at it the other way round – are good card-players always successful in their professional lives? Hardly.

Sam was an intelligent and prosperous man, a keen pupil in a recent Beginners' class of mine. He soon grasped the elements of Acol bidding, and he and his partner began to bid some creditable contracts. However, when Sam was declarer, the result was invariably a disaster.

I began to watch him as he played a hand, and it became clear that Sam had a deep-rooted aversion to taking out trumps. When I reminded him of what I'd told the class about Victor Mollo's awful warning to those who do not lead trumps at the first opportunity (that they would end up sleeping on the Embankment) he looked blank. Apparently he had missed that lesson.

"That explains it," he said. "Do you know, I've never actually made one single contract since I've been in the class. But I'm sure I will now that I know about taking out trumps."

I forbore to mention that the importance of taking out trumps had been stressed more than once during the course, and watched Sam and partner bid this hand to 6♣.

	Sam	Partner
♠	4	A 9 2
♡	K Q J 9	A 6 5
◊	K	6 5 3 2
♣	A J 9 8 5 3 2	K Q 10

It was a fine contract. The ◊A was led and defender switched to a trump. There were twelve tricks for the taking. "A piece of cake," I said. "The first contract you're going to make is a slam – not a bad start! But don't forget what I said about trumps . . ."

"I must play trumps," he said.

Somebody was calling for help from another table. "I'll leave you to it," I told him.

Five minutes later I was back at Sam's table, scratching my head in disbelief. "You *can't* have gone three light!" I exclaimed. "You've got one spade, seven clubs and four hearts. You let them make their small trumps, didn't you? You didn't take out trumps!"

"I most certainly did!" Sam retorted indignantly. "Didn't I?" he appealed to his partner. "No doubt about it," partner confirmed.

The hand had been played duplicate fashion. I asked the participants to pick up their cards. "Play it again, Sam," I said. "I want to know how you can avoid making twelve tricks. I'll bet you can't do it this time."

I was wrong. The ◇A was led once more, and Sam won the trump continuation. Then, with an expression of deep virtue on his face, he proceeded to play six more rounds of clubs. After the third round he paused, looking for discards from dummy. On the fourth and fifth club he threw two small spades; on the sixth and seventh he threw two small hearts . . . yes, nine tricks was not only possible, it was inevitable. He cashed dummy's two bare Aces and turned to me. "What did I do wrong?" he demanded.

"You played the trumps out," I said. *"That's* what went wrong . . ."

"But you told me . . ."

Gently I explained. "Oh, I see!" he said when I had finished. "You never need to play out trumps when the opponents have run out of them. That's *always* the case, is it? No exceptions?"

The thought of trump squeezes briefly crossed my mind. Then I considered how long it might be before Sam started on squeezes. There would be ample time to put him right.

"No exceptions," I promised.

EAVESDROPPINGS

"Director, please," stage-whispered a lady. "I've just led a small trump from dummy and put the Ace on it, and no-one has followed suit. Someone's revoked!"

The Club Director did a quick tour of the table.

"Have another count up," he advised. "I think you've got all thirteen!"

Keith Jarrett

SMITH PETERS (OR WHY YOU WIN AT BRIDGE)

by Paul Hackett

How many weapons do you have in your armoury which are indispensable? Imagine bidding without using Stayman or Blackwood (albeit in some hybrid form). May I add another to your list? 'Ah!' you say, 'It must be the Hackett convention.' No, it is not – although I might add that that is a useful convention against Weak Twos. The gadget I find difficult to live without is the *Smith Peter*, sometimes known as the *Smith Echo*.

'What on earth,' you ask yourself, 'is this madman trying to inject into us now?' Well, the Smith Peter is not a bidding convention, but a special play of the cards.

It is the play of an unnecessary high card on the first lead by declarer to say we liked your lead or our lead. When does it apply? I recommend that you only play Smith Peters against no-trumps.

Now I will shock ye olde conservatives even more by suggesting that you play Smith Peters on both sides of the table. Thus you can tell your partner 'I liked your/my lead' or 'Please switch to another suit.'

What on earth am I talking about? Well, here are some examples. You lead the 6 from A-10-8-6-3 ('Ah!' you say, 'I don't lead fourth best, I lead the 3' – well, so be it), partner plays the Jack, and declarer the King. Who has the Queen? While we know that many of you are experts at finding the lady, we mere mortals have a problem, but Smith Peters come to our rescue. When declarer leads, we rush in with the highest card we can afford, so if we had A-8-2 we would play the 8 and look with anticipation at partner's card. If partner plays a small card, we know declarer has the Queen, so we have to find a way of getting partner in; but if partner plays a high card we have manna from heaven and know that we can continue the suit.

Here is another example. We hear Right-Hand Opponent open 1♡ and this is our hand:

♠ 9 2
♡ A Q 10 8 3
♢ A Q 5
♣ 10 9 8

'What a stupid fellow,' we think, 'he has taken the words right out of my mouth' – so, reluctantly, we pass. On our left comes 1♠, and 1NT on our right closes the auction.

We elect to lead the ♣10. Declarer wins and leads a spade. We play the ♠2: 'Please, please, switch partner!'

Is there any time we do not Smith Peter? Yes, when dummy has a long suit with no entry and we need to give count. What if we have a singleton? Then we Smith Peter at the next trick and hope that partner can work it out.

Are there any other advantages? Yes, we can now lead small from bad suits (this may take some getting used to).

Below is a spectacular hand where Smith Peters really paid dividends.

```
           North
           ♠ 10 7 5
           ♡ A K 10 9 3
           ◇ 5 2
           ♣ A 7 4
West                    East
♠ K J 3                 ♠ 9 8 2
♡ 7 6 5                 ♡ Q J 8
◇ 10 4 3                ◇ J 9 8 7
♣ K J 8 3               ♣ 10 9 5
           South
           ♠ A Q 6 4
           ♡ 4 2
           ◇ A K Q 6
           ♣ Q 6 2
```

Because we played Smith Peters, the ♡5 was led against 3NT by South, covered by the 9 and the Jack – declarer contributing the ♡2. The ♣10 produced the Queen, the King, and the 4. The ♣J was continued; dummy ducked again, but was forced to win the Ace on the next round. Declarer played a diamond to his hand, then led a heart and put in the ♡10. When the smoke had cleared, declarer was three down. Could you honestly say that you would have done better?

At the recent Olympiad, virtually every pair played Smith Peters. Come on in, join the in-crowd, and you will wonder how you survived so long without Smith Peters, but please – please, don't play them against me.

PARTNERSHIP (MISS) UNDERSTANDING

She was a sweet young thing, about 12-years old, and she had been brought down to the club by her father, a regular member, to play in her first tournament. She obviously felt very grown up, and her conduct and play were both correct and good.

At the third table, the opponents arrived in a 4♠ contract. Her father led, and as soon as his card was face up on the table, the S.Y.T. displayed her alert card. Puzzled, declarer sought enlightenment.

"It's singleton," was the prompt reply.

On further enquiry as to how she knew, the S.Y.T. explained with perfect composure: "He led with his left hand. Anything else, he always leads with his right!"

Richard Kent

PREMEDITATED MURDER

by David Perkins

My team-of-eight was playing its final match in the county league. At the start, both teams had an equal chance of winning it, but the final result (11–1 VPS to our opponents) meant that our interest in the championship title was finished! In spite of the outcome of the match, one hand remains memorable.

When a player murders the defence to a hand, it is often through failure to give enough thought to the correct line. On this occasion, East gave the situation careful consideration, but came up with the wrong answer.

	North	Dealer: West
	♠ J 4 2	Game All
	♡ A 8 5 3	
	◇ K 9 4	
	♣ Q 10 3	
West		East
♠ 7 6		♠ K 10 3
♡ 10 9 4		♡ K Q 2
◇ 10 6		◇ A 8 5 2
♣ J 7 6 5 4 2		♣ K 9 8
	South	
	♠ A Q 9 8 5	
	♡ J 7 6	
	◇ Q J 7 3	
	♣ A	

The bidding:

West	North	East	South
NB	NB	1NT	2♠
NB	3♠	NB	4♠
NB	NB	NB	

West led the ◇10, covered by the King and Ace, and West returned a diamond won by dummy's 9. After some thought, South led a small spade from dummy, finessed the Queen, and cashed the ♠A – hoping to find East with ♠K-x. When the ♠K failed to appear, South led the ♡6 towards the Ace and West did well to insert the ♡9. Declarer played small from dummy, and East gave the situation a very studied review. Eventually, she overtook with her ♡Q, cashed the ♠K, and exited with a diamond.

Declarer now cashed his last diamond and a trump, leaving this position:

	North	
	♠ —	
	♡ A 8	
	◇ —	
	♣ Q 10	
West		East
♠ —		♠ —
♡ 10 4		♡ K 2
◇ —		◇ —
♣ J 7		♣ K 9
	South	
	♠ 8	
	♡ J 7	
	◇ —	
	♣ A	

On the last trump, North discarded a heart and East was caught in a criss-cross squeeze. Once again she thought long and hard before selecting her card. But whichever card she chose, South was in control. Eventually, she let go a club. So South cashed his ♣A and took the last two tricks with the ♡A and the ♣Q. Had a heart been discarded, South would have cashed the ♡A and taken the last two tricks with the ♣A and ♡J.

"Could I have done better?" East asked her partner.

"If you let me win with the nine of hearts, I can play a second heart to break up the squeeze," West replied.

North said nothing, but leaned across the table to shake his partner's hand.

PROBLEMS
OF A BRIDGE ORGANISER

by Graham Jepson

As a shared proprietary-club owner with my wife Pat, I decided to run bridge holidays and outside-club events when our search for our own club premises proved fruitless. Once a decision to hold an outside-club event has been made, problems exist from the word go.

The venue must have good parking, up to the front door for everyone. The room must be spacious, no stairs to it unless there is a lift (but if there is a lift, there must be stairs too). Bridge tables, unless you bring your own, should be square – rectangular may have to do. Chairs should be comfortable, arm-less – unless you like arms.

The room should be well lit; strip lights are best, but hotel chandeliers may have to do. Bulbs are often absent or indeed not wholly operational. Carpets make the floor more attractive and make for a quieter atmosphere – unless the venue is a countryside hotel alongside dog kennels on a Bank Holiday.

Extractor fans should not disturb the concentration of the players. Smoke should not irritate the eyes of the non-smokers – inability to smoke should not distress the nerves of the smokers. The room should be neither too hot, nor too cold, neither draughty, nor airless.

The meal chosen, well in advance, for the competitors should reflect the unpredictability of the English climate: salad on a hot day, hot meal on a cold day. Drinks should be on tap all day.

The date you have chosen should not clash with any other local bridge event, nor, if at all possible, with any national sport . The prizes chosen should be suited to who- ever wins, regardless of age, sex, or class; they should be tasteful, thoughtful, and include drink or vouchers. You have to try and get it right.

The scorecards, travellers, curtain cards, silent bidders, table covers, boards and table numbers are easy to stack alongside the prizes in the

Graham and Pat Jepson

car boot, together with a change of clothes. The Local Points books take pride of place in the briefcase.

Starting time, formerly 2.00 p.m., is being changed to an earlier start to give an earlier finishing time. Will the players remember? Starting time is upon us. The bulk of the players arrive in the nick of time. Where to put coats? Where is the cloakroom? Am I North-South? How are you, dear? Seats are taken. It's time. One pair missing. Are they late? Have they forgotten the date? Any reserves? I shouldn't have to sit out!

Announcements are read out after the initial welcome. Play is about to commence. All is quiet.

"Darling, have we brought the boards with us?"

Club Bridge

LUCKILY IT WAS DUPLICATE!
by Harold Schogger

Harold Schogger invites you to the

77 BRIDGE CLUB

81a, Brent St., Hendon, London NW4 2DY
Telephone 081-202 4718

This hand produced some remarkable scores in a recent duplicate session held at the **77 Bridge Club** – from North's sacrifice in 6♡ doubled making to East-West bidding, and making, 6♠ despite the spades breaking 4–0.

South should open with a pre-emptive bid in hearts, and after some sort of take-out bid by West North's best course of action is to make an advance sacrifice of 6♡ to stop East-West finding their best contract.

Should West lead his ♠A, declarer will be able to establish dummy's Queen for a club discard, so making an improbable contract.

If the East-West partnership play in spades, then declarer should assume that South is more likely to have a spade shortage, and therefore the ♠A must be cashed first to guard against four spades being held by North. This good technique will mean that North's spades can be finessed for just one loser, so bringing the contract home.

If this hand had occurred in a teams' match, it may well have resulted in a double slam swing!

```
                North            Dealer: South
                ♠ Q J 8 6        Game All
                ♡ K 10 5 4 2
                ◇ —
                ♣ 8 5 4 3
West                             East
♠ A 7 5 4                        ♠ K 10 9 3 2
♡ —                              ♡ 9
◇ A Q J 10 9 5 2                 ◇ 6 4
♣ K 7                            ♣ A Q J 10 6
                South
                ♠ —
                ♡ A Q J 8 7 6 3
                ◇ K 8 7 3
                ♣ 9 2
```

THE BANANA GAME
by Neal Cutler

"One more rubber?" I enquired of my Left-Hand Opponent. It was already 12.30 a.m. I was playing with my wife, Linda; we were just eight units down, and one last effort might clear it. Anyway, it would not be easy to get to sleep. The ship was bouncing on the sea more than at any other time I could recall. This was our first-ever Bridge cruise, and we were enjoying it to the full. First-class cabins, sumptuous food, decidedly attractive waitresses, and as much bridge as one could accommodate. In the morning we would finally be arriving in Perth, Australia. My good lady wife was looking forward to dragging me off the boat to accompany her on a shopping expedition in the local . . . THUD! . . .

The most almighty noise reverberated through the ship as we were all flung off our seats in the direction of the band playing at the top end of the floor. Sirens rang out. Pandemonium spread. We had obviously hit something and the boat was tilting. I seemed to recall that the lifeboats were found on the portside of the upper deck, but could I get there? . . .

The sun was blazing down as I slowly opened my eyes, but where was I? The waves lapped against my legs as I lay on the shore of what seemed to be a desert island. I was shipwrecked. "Andy, is that you?" I looked up, and running towards me was Linda, with a man and a woman. "Thank God you're safe," she exclaimed, as we hugged each other. She introduced me to Roger and Justine, her newly-made acquaintances, and said that they had scoured the island, which was about two miles in circumference, and that the place was deserted. "What about food?" I asked. "Well, we found some fruit growing inland; here, have some." I was certainly very hungry and grabbed a couple of bananas from the man's outstretched hand. "Thanks, Roger," I muttered as I gorged myself on the proffered food.

We began to reconcile ourselves to our predicament, and it wasn't too long before we got a game up on the shore, banking some sand as a table, and drying out a pack of cards which I still had in my pocket from before the collision. I began by partnering my wife, and the first rubber passed innocuously enough. The standard was not particularly high, and we were just totting up the score when a disembodied voice came forth . . .

"That's sand-mound up, I believe." The four of us looked round still not seeing who was responsible for this interruption. We suddenly noticed some distinct rustling from an overlooking palm tree. We gazed expectantly. From the bottom of the tree emerged a monkey, about three feet tall, who strutted towards our game with an engaging smile.

"You don't mind if I cut in, do you?"

"Not at all," I responded boldly on behalf of the human element. "Fresh er . . . blood . . . is always welcome," I went on. I cut the most hirsute of the group, while Linda partnered Justine.

As I dealt the cards, the monkey interjected: "Let us play a strong no-trump, forcing twos, Fishbein over threes, Stayman, and Basic Acol."

"I normally use the weak no-trump," I demurred.

"My friend," the monkey replied, "the strong no-trump is played in all the big banana games on this island."

I sorted my cards and immediately regretted that we were not playing a weak no-trump, since I held this hand:

South
♠ J 7 4
♡ K Q 10 6
◊ A J 6
♣ Q 9 6

"One heart," I opened. Linda passed. The monkey scanned his hand and condescendingly bid 4♡, which closed the auction. My wife led the ◊3 and the monkey tabled his hand while muttering: "I think I should have enough for you".

This was the full deal:

The Monkey
♠ K 8
♡ A J 9 4
◊ 10 2
♣ A J 10 4 2

Linda
♠ 10 6 5
♡ 5 3
◊ K 9 8 4 3
♣ 8 5 3

Justine
♠ A Q 9 3 2
♡ 8 7 2
◊ Q 7 5
♣ K 7

Me
♠ J 7 4
♡ K Q 10 6
◊ A J 6
♣ Q 9 6

I surveyed dummy's cards. I mused to myself that partner might have bid 2♣ over my heart, initially hoping for more than a game. Anyway, the final contract would be the same.

Prospects looked quite good. I only needed the ♣K or the ♠A well placed to make the contract. East played the ◊Q over dummy's ◊2, and I won with the Ace. After drawing trumps I took the club finesse. East won the ♣K and put West in with the ◊K. Now the spade switch defeated the contract.

"Everything was wrong," I grumbled.

"Especially your line of play," retorted the monkey. "You had no need for two diamond tricks, it was far more important to keep West off the lead. If you allow East to hold the first trick with the Queen of diamonds, the defence can make only a diamond, a club, and a spade."

'Of course, he's right', I reflected as I cut the cards for the next hand. A little forethought at trick one would have guaranteed the contract against any lie of the key cards. The monkey was clearly a very experienced player. He proceeded to wrap up the rubber in two hands, first with the help of a 'momma-poppa elimination throw-in', as he put it, and subsequently with a squeeze without the count.

The monkey made some excuse about the time, got up, thanked us for the game, and went off towards the interior. When he had gone about ten feet, he turned round, his face still garlanded with a broad smile.

"You would all be very welcome at our bridge club on the other side of the island," he called out. "The beginners' classes are on Wednesdays!"

People and Bridge

'LITTLE CLUB' IN GERMANY

by Harry Liley

For several years I was a member of a club in Cologne, where Acol was played and Acol courses held. Although this system is played in cosmopolitan and expert circles, my later experience in the town of Kerpen-Sindorf shows that the predominant system in Germany is the 'Little Club'.

The reason for its popularity is socio-structural. There are thousands of small bridge groups in Germany, frequently formed around a bridge teacher. They are not bridge clubs as such, but simply people who were taught and remained in the group to continue playing, or who left to form their own groups. The members are over 90% female and, in general, first learned to play bridge at middle age or later. I myself play in four different groups where I am the only male!

The Little Club is comparatively easy to learn, and one can become an average player in a short time. This is an important factor, as most of the players learned bridge for social reasons, and learning does not come easy after the age of forty. The system allows for flexibility, and it is possible to play variations appropriate to your partner of the day. For example, I seldom use the forcing 2♣ (23+ points), preferring to open 1♣ (12+) and jump-bid over partner's response. This paid dividends a few weeks ago when my partner, having all four Aces and 26 points, opened 1♣. I replied 2◊ (at least five diamonds and 10 points), whereupon partner leapt to 7NT (making, of course)!

My own introduction to Contract Bridge resulted from an over-zealous Duty Officer confiscating cards and money from a Solo game on board a troopship on the way to Hong Kong in 1938. A kindly-disposed ship's officer told us to claim that we had been playing bridge, which – he said – was not punishable as it was a game of skill. I was fascinated, and have been ever since.

Like most members of my 'little clubs', I have never played Tournament Bridge. I nevertheless take the game seriously – it provides me with much pleasure and human experience. It is not, however, a matter of life and death!

WHICH STAYMAN, PARTNER?
by Ron Heath

"I only play Basic Acol, no conventions – well, Stayman and Blackwood!"

The above well-worn introductory conversation at the bridge table is often heard – with the implied comment that conventions are of no advantage. Maybe so; but is *your* Stayman the same as your opponents'? More to the point, is it the same as your partner's?

In spite of the nowadays clear statements by the English Bridge Union that Stayman *is* alertable, there are still many occasions when it is not alerted. Failure to alert, when an alert is due, is defined as *mis-information*, with possible consequential damage to opponents. If the opponents are not damaged by the failure to alert, the Tournament Director will not apply any adjustments to the score.

♠ A K x x
♡ A K x x
◇ A K x x
♣ x

Now look at this hand. In fourth position, non-Vulnerable vs. Vulnerable opponents, holding the hand on the left, you hear the following bidding:

LHO	Partner	RHO	You
1NT (a)	NB	2♣ (b)	?
(a) Stated as 12–14.			
(b) Not alerted.			

You pass, and expect to pick up a 200 or even a 500 penalty in due course. Hard luck! This is the end of the auction, and you have got a bottom.

The 2♣ bid was a weakness take-out into clubs, and since the opponents *don't* play Stayman (it's true: some people don't) they did not alert. The room is playing at the 3-level; but your opponents were able to stop at the two level.

Why don't they play Stayman? Could it be that their 1NT opener denies a 4-card major? If this is the case, then naturally they don't have to look for a 4–4 fit! This should certainly be on their convention card, which should have been brought to your attention at the start of the round.

Call the Director.

No doubt he will be a bit perplexed as to what to do – unless he is well-versed in the latest details of the Directives. In this case it is simple: he will tell you that you too have a duty to find out about the opponents' 2♣ reply to 1NT *before* the start of a round. So he should not do anything to alter the score.

Let us return to another aspect of Stayman, one which is going to split you, the readers, into several camps! Suppose you make an opening 1NT on a good 13-count with four cards in both majors. Your partner bids 2♣, you tap the table and bid . . . Well, what do you bid?

Reference to *All about Acol* by Cohen and Lederer advises that the response is 2♠ (with the implication that this reply does not deny four hearts). However, this book also contains a footnote to the effect that tournament players nowadays bid 2♡ (with the implication that there may still be a 4-card spade suit in the hand). Alternatively, some of you may favour a 2NT reply. In my opinion the majority would bid 2♡.

Let us assume the 2♡ bid. Partner now bids 3NT.

No doubt you are thinking, 'Partner doesn't have a heart fit, but he used Stayman so we should have a spade fit; do I now bid 4♠?' The crunch is whether you *know* – not just *assume* – that the Stayman bidder has at least one 4-card major. *If* that is your firm agreement, then bid 4♠. Before you run off to your partner and make this a firm agreement, might I suggest you read on.

♠ K x
♡ x x
♦ K Q J 10 x x
♣ A J x

We could all construct hands where a Stayman bid is worthwhile; but the hand does *not* contain a 4-card major. Consider the hand on the left.

This looks like a good chance at 3NT if opposite a weak 1NT opener, provided the opponents do not cash five or even six hearts. So why not use Stayman to see if the 1NT bidder has a 4-card heart suit? If he does, then you can bid 3NT with more confidence. The sequence is thus 1NT – 2♣ – 2♡ – 3NT – End. That's what *you* think! Now partner takes it out into 4♠. Your plan has failed – unless you have agreed with your partner that a Stayman bid does *not* promise a 4-card major.

At this stage, the key point is to be aware that Stayman is an *asking* bid, it does not *show* anything – it was never designed to show, nor is it licensed to show. Players have just assumed that it is easier to bid that way.

So, next, we need to look at bidding which takes the guesswork out of the spade fit or no spade fit. The key to the partnership bidding is to remember that the Stayman 2♣ bidder is in control of the auction. It is up to him to remove the doubt by using a simple partnership-agreed system.

The simple system that I would advocate is summarised by the phrase *Never ever miss out a 4-card major.* So the Stayman bidder, having heard partner's 2♡ response and being aware that there may still be a 4-card spade suit in the opener's hand, should bid 2♠ (invitational) or 3♠ (forcing) depending on his strength, just as he would bid 2 or 3NT depending on his strength. Now opener retains control: if he does not hold four spades, he converts to 2NT or 3NT; if he does hold four spades, he either passes or raises to 4♠ or bids 3NT according to the strength of his hand.

Don't forget, if you have found a heart fit, the preceding paragraph is redundant.

The corollary of all this is that if responder holds both majors and a weak hand, he must reply 2♠ to partner's opening bid of 1NT. The big drawback is that now the chance of playing at the 2-level with a 4-4 heart fit is lost. Still, one cannot have everything in life!

SICILIAN INTERLUDE
by Maureen Dennison

The third Super Bowl was played last year in Mondello, Sicily. Eight top international teams, together with a journalist and the President of the relevant Bridge Union (and spouse) were invited as guests, air travel as well as hotel expenses being fully paid. The teams were drawn into two pools and played a round robin of 24-board matches. The quality of the field ensured that this was an event worth winning. The moving force behind the event was Aldo Borzi, a leading Sicilian businessman, and he had wonderful support and sponsorship from the Palermo Regional Tourist Board.

Great Britain was represented by Gus Calderwood, Dick Shek, Brian Senior and Peter Czerniewski. They were drawn against France, whom they beat 25–5; the Netherlands, to whom they lost 14–16; and Italy. This last team played inspired bridge, and we were trounced 24–6. However, our total score was just enough to be second and earn a place in the finals. In the other pool, a fine Polish team beat all opponents for first place; Sweden was second, having lost also to Austria 12–18, but beating Greece 21–9, so both second-placed teams had won only one match out of three!

So in the semifinal we faced Poland, who continued to impress. We had chances, but they ran out the winners by 34 IMPs. The other match between Italy and Sweden was a see-saw event, with Italy in a commanding position by board 19, leading 50–25. Over the last five boards they gained 5 and lost 46 IMPs. They missed one slam, bid 6NT failing when Sweden bid 6♥ making on a finesse, missed a game and then took a phantom sacrifice which cost 950 points!

So the final was to be between Poland and Sweden. Perhaps it is unfair to pick out a board which was bad for Poland, as they played magnificent bridge throughout, but it always gives hope to us lesser mortals when top players make an elementary mistake. Look at the deal overleaf.

The winners of the Super Bowl

This was the bidding in the two rooms:

OPEN:

South	West	North	East
Gothe	*Zmudzinski*	*Lindqvist*	*Balicki*
NB	4♡	4♠	5♡
5♠	NB	6♠	All Pass

Lindqvist for Sweden had no problem in the play and scored +980.

CLOSED:

South	West	North	East
Blat	*Bjerregard*	*Wilcosz*	*Morath*
3♣	3♡	4♠	5♡
5♠	6♡	Dbl	All Pass

This contract went the obvious two down for minus 300. We have all been taught not to pre-empt in front of partner with a bad suit, especially when the hand also contains a good major-suit holding. The ♠Q-8-4 *and* the singleton heart make the hand too powerful to open 3♣. When it came to the high-level decision, North could not believe that his partner could have the right cards for 6♠.

	North	Dealer: South
	♠ A K J 5 3 2	Love All
	♡ 6 4	
	♢ A K Q J 10	
	♣ —	
West		*East*
♠ 10 9 6		♠ 7
♡ A K Q 9 8 5 2		♡ J 10 3
♢ 5 3		♢ 9 8 4 2
♣ 6		♣ A Q 10 9 2
	South	
	♠ Q 8 4	
	♡ 7	
	♢ 7 6	
	♣ K J 8 7 5 4 3	

This board was uncharacteristic, and the Poles earned twice as many swings as Sweden, running out winners with a score of 83–57 IMPs.

The teams then crossed the island to Cefalù (super for Christmas shopping, especially knitwear and leather) to take part in an open Italian congress from Thursday to Sunday. We played three sessions each of Pairs and

The runners-up

Swiss Teams. For those of you who fancy a trip abroad, it is wonderful value and a most interesting experience. All-in hotel, including wine and water at meals, and a Saturday-night Sicilian banquet (fantastic: a buffet of twenty-five cold and fifteen hot dishes, salads and fish, pastas and meat followed by puddings and fruit) was little over £110 for twin accommodation and £135 single. Special discounts are available if booking through *Borzi Viaggi, via Serradifalco 2c, 90145 Palermo; telephone 01039 91 225511.* There are numerous high value and special category prizes – ladies, mixed, etc. – and the array of cups and awards has to be seen to be believed, even though the entry fees are quite modest.

However, one must be prepared to play teams Italian style. They live at a different pace from us, and are happy to chat between rounds and wait three-quarters of an hour for their re-assignments, to start play at 2 p.m. and finish around 3 a.m. I found the whole event most enjoyable and a wonderful experience.

THE SEVEN OF DIAMONDS
by Ian Reissmann

The bridge-playing world of my acquaintance is divided into two groups: those who can guess the subject matter of this article from its title; and those who cannot. For readers whose bridge-playing life remains unlit by this little diversion, I shall explain. The object of the game is to win the last trick with the seven of diamonds, where diamonds must not be trumps.

You can usually tell those who are playing the 'Seven of Diamonds' game because, when they are declarer, they will suddenly start giving the hand extra thought at about trick eight, well before triumphantly playing to trick thirteen.

Although this sounds a relatively trivial subgame, it can cause quite curious problems. Getting trumps out of the way and disentangling entries can lead to quite new and different plays from those familiar to most players. I can remember one team-mate embarking on a seemingly pointless cross-ruff and suit establishment, in order to make the seven of diamonds at trick thirteen. A non-material dummy reversal – eat your hearts out, Kelsey and Otlik!

The following hand shows an example of what can be required to engineer the seven-of-diamonds coup, and also provides some food for thought on how to defend against a declarer playing the game.

West	North	East	South
1◊	1♠	2♡	3♠
4♡	All Pass		

North — Dealer: West — Love All
- ♠ Q J 10 2
- ♡ 5 4
- ◊ Q 5 4
- ♣ K 6 4 3

West
- ♠ K 3
- ♡ A Q 2
- ◊ A K 7 3
- ♣ Q 9 7 5

East
- ♠ A 7 6 5 4
- ♡ K J 10 9 2
- ◊ 10 9 2
- ♣ —

South
- ♠ 9 8
- ♡ 8 7 6
- ◊ J 8 6
- ♣ A J 10 8 2

The bidding was straightforward, as long as you regard the pre-emptive raising of a suit in which your side has the minority in both length and strength as normal. However Mason and Bentley (for it was they) have certainly never lacked courage. After a spade lead declarer, managing to avoid looking surprised at dummy, played King, Ace and ruffed a spade (South discarding a diamond) before pausing for thought. "You've got the seven of diamonds there," said Rick Mason to declarer, who appeared puzzled, whereupon the rules of 'Seven of Diamonds' were explained to him. Declarer played the ♡Q to the King, ruffed his fourth spade with the Ace of trumps, ruffed a club and then drew trumps and cashed the last spade, throwing clubs from dummy.

The position now was:

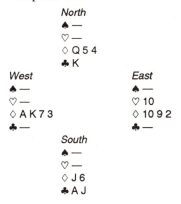

North
♠ —
♡ —
◇ Q 5 4
♣ K

West
♠ —
♡ —
◇ A K 7 3
♣ —

East
♠ —
♡ 10
◇ 10 9 2
♣ —

South
♠ —
♡ —
◇ J 6
♣ A J

East now ran the ◇10 to North, who won and returned a club which declarer ruffed, discarding the ◇K from dummy. Then came the ◇9 to the Ace, and the seven of diamonds at trick thirteen.

This was – as Kelsey would say – an instructive hand. Declarer could never win the seven of diamonds without some help from the defence. Certainly South should keep his diamonds, but did you spot North's mistake at the end? If he returns a diamond, declarer is locked in dummy and cannot avoid playing his trump at trick thirteen!

TEST YOUR DECLARER PLAY AT TEAMS

by Bob Rowlands

PROBLEM 1:

West	East
♠ Q 8 5 3	♠ A 10 9 6 2
♡ K J 5 4	♡ 6 2
◇ K J 2	◇ A 10 7 3
♣ 3 2	♣ A K

You are East, declarer in 4♠ at Love All. South leads the ♣4 to North's ♣Q and your Ace. You cash the ♠A, ♣K, and lead a spade to South's King, North following suit. Now South leads the ♡3. Your play.

PROBLEM 2:

West	East
♠ K J 9 5	♠ A Q 10 7 4 3
♡ A K Q 7 4	♡ 6 2
◇ A 7	◇ Q 8 4
♣ A 5	♣ K Q

At Game All, you (East) are declarer in 7♠. South leads the ♣J. How do you play to make sure of your contract?
(Trumps break 2–1, and North shows out on the second round.)

PROBLEM 3:

North
♠ 7 4
♡ J
◇ K 7 6 5 4
♣ 10 6 4 3 2

South
♠ A K
♡ A K 2
◇ Q 8 3
♣ A J 8 7 5

You are South, vulnerable, and declarer in 3NT. West leads the ♠10, and East follows with the ♠8. Plan the play.

PROBLEM 4:

North
♠ J 5 4
♡ 10 8 7 6
◇ A K 3
♣ 8 6 2

South
♠ Q 9 6
♡ A K Q J 9 5
◇ J 10 8
♣ A

Game All. You are South, declarer in 4♡. Plan the play on the lead of the ♣Q.
(Solutions on page 121.)

67

TWO LOSERS MAKE ONE WINNER

by Lynne Heath

The more exotic parts of the world are usually associated with the name **Mercian Bridge**; but the regular winter holiday in Torremolinos has become very popular. Last year it attracted players from the U.S.A. as well as Scotland, Ireland, and England. It was thus decided to stage an 'International' for the last two days, when most guests played in the ever popular Swiss Teams.

Ireland and U.S.A. met in the last round with scores separated by 2 VPs, both having won their previous matches. They were both good teams, and the match aroused much interest. This was one of the hands that gave Ireland victory.

The Irish South became declarer in 6♡ and received the ♠Q lead. There had been no bidding from East-West, but the declarer deduced from the opening lead that the ♠A was with East. He reasoned that his contract was safe if trumps broke 2–2 and diamonds no worse than 4–1; should the trumps break 3–1, then he would need a 3–2 diamond break.

```
              North
              ♠ K 3 2
              ♡ 9 7 2
              ◇ Q 7 6
              ♣ Q 8 6 2
West                      East
♠ Q J 5 4                 ♠ A 10 9 8 7 6
♡ 5                       ♡ 10 8 3
◇ J 10 9 8                ◇ 5
♣ J 9 7 3                 ♣ K 5 4
              South
              ♠ —
              ♡ A K Q J 6 4
              ◇ A K 4 3 2
              ♣ A 10
```

At trick one, declarer played a low spade from dummy and ruffed in hand. Two rounds of trumps revealed the 3–1 break. Now the ◇A-K followed, East discarding a low spade on the second round. Why, since he could have ruffed?

The astute declarer reasoned that East held the ♣K as well as the ♠A and did not want to be thrown in. In fact, a club or a spade lead from East would have given declarer his twelfth trick.

Accordingly, declarer played a diamond to dummy's Queen, which

Lynne Heath relaxing in the January sun with husband Ron.

```
      North
      ♠ —
      ♡ 9
      ◇ —
      ♣ Q 8 6 2
West              East
♠ J               ♠ A
♡ —               ♡ 10
◇ —               ◇ —
♣ J 9 7 3         ♣ K 5 4
      South
      ♠ —
      ♡ Q J
      ◇ 2
      ♣ A 10
```

held; a small spade ruffed in hand; then a fourth diamond discarding the ♠K (loser on loser play). Note that if he ruffed in dummy, East can overruff and exit safely with the ♠A.

The end position is shown on the left.

West was hopelessly endplayed. If he led the ♠J, he would give declarer a ruff and a discard; so he led a club, hoping that declarer would get it wrong. But South played low in dummy and his losing club became a winner and his twelfth trick.

Mercian Bridge

OUT OF A TIGHT CORNER

by Jean Standish

Here is an example of how to get out of a tight corner which occurred during an overseas Mercian Bridge Holiday.

Playing in pairs against Turkish opposition I ended up in a doubful 4♠ contract as South, rather than in a possible 5♣. The defence began with two rounds of diamonds, then East switched to a small heart. How would you continue?

```
      North
      ♠ 10 8 7
      ♡ 5 4 2
      ◇ 6 5
      ♣ J 9 8 7 2
West                East
♠ J 6 5 3           ♠ 4 2
♡ J 9 8             ♡ Q 10 7 6
◇ K Q 10 3          ◇ A J 9 7 4
♣ 6 5               ♣ 4 3
      South
      ♠ A K Q 9
      ♡ A K 3
      ◇ 8 2
      ♣ A K Q 10
```

The best play for declarer is to win with the ♡A, and then play one top trump followed by the *nine* of trumps. The defence are now powerless. Unless declarer ducks a trump early, West can ruff the fourth round of clubs to ensure that declarer loses a heart.

This play protects declarer from a diamond force, because dummy still has a trump, and allows all trumps to be drawn before cashing clubs.

AN OLD-FASHIONED DOUBLE

by Sam Jones

A timid young man called Roy Hudd,
Whose leads were his fourth best and MUD,
Said: "I'm still in some doubt,
Is your double for take-out?"
My partner replied: "It's for blood!"

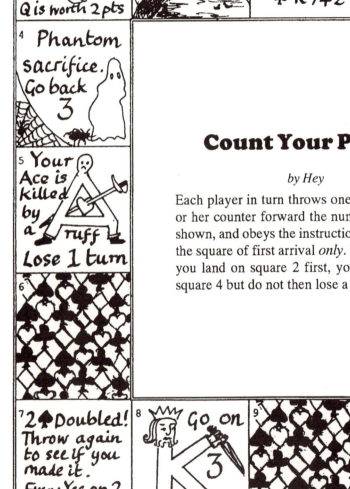

3 Go on **2**

Q is worth 2 pts

2 Throw again

1 START HERE
♠ A 2
♡ K J 6
◇ Q J 9 6
♣ K 7 4 2

4 Phantom sacrifice. Go back **3**

5 Your Ace is killed by a ruff. Lose 1 turn

6

Count Your Points

by Hey

Each player in turn throws one die, moves his or her counter forward the number of squares shown, and obeys the instructions – if any – on the square of first arrival *only*. For example, if you land on square 2 first, you go on two to square 4 but do not then lose a turn.

7 2♠ Doubled! Throw again to see if you made it. Even: Yes, on 2 Odd: No, back 2

8 Go on **3** K is worth 3 pts

9

10 You are caught in a..... Lose 1 turn

70

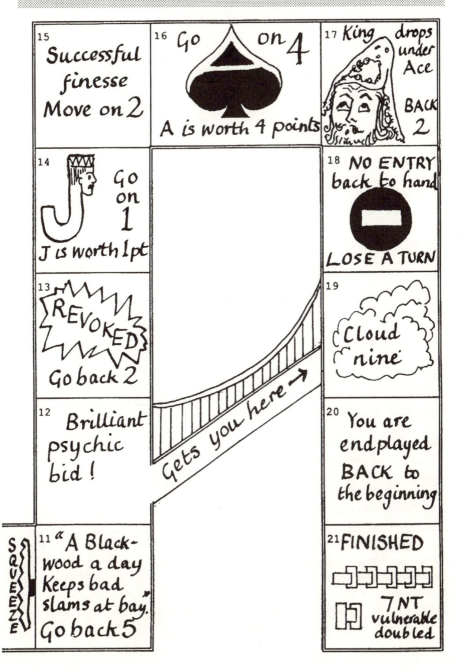

15 Successful finesse Move on 2

16 Go on 4 — A is worth 4 points

17 King drops under Ace BACK 2

14 Go on 1 — J is worth 1pt

18 NO ENTRY back to hand — LOSE A TURN

13 REVOKED Go back 2

19 Cloud nine

Gets you here →

12 Brilliant psychic bid !

20 You are endplayed BACK to the beginning

11 "A Blackwood a day Keeps bad slams at bay." Go back 5

SQUEEZE

21 FINISHED — 7 NT vulnerable doubled

PRE-EMPT

by Steve Sharrock

Betty had opened three diamonds
With eight cards up to the Queen,
Penny had doubled for take-out
When Steve made a bold 'intervene.'
Five clubs he bid without blinking
Not holding the Ace or the King
So Bar with nine cards in the majors
Was left with a 'guess bid', poor thing.

Five hearts and 4 spades had Bar noted
With quite a few points on the side.
A small slam in hearts should be easy
But a grand rather hard to decide.
Not wanting to be ostentatious
But needing to get in the act
She jumped to six hearts so that Penny
Could bid the final contract.

Betty passed as expected
For she had no more to say
And Penny with Ace-King of diamonds
Was certain the grand slam would play.
"Seven hearts", whispered Penny
Assured that Bar's bid would be sound.
All eyes then turned on to Stephen
Whose double was easily found.

Bar did not change the bidding
For she hoped to make all the tricks.
A truly fast-flowing sequence
But it should have ended in six.
It wasn't a very good contract
For six no-trumps was stone cold
But pre-emptive bidding adds pressure
We all are reliably told.

Betty continued by passing
Then looked for a lead from her hand
And selected the five spot of diamonds
As a means of defeating the grand.
Penny was pleased to be dummy
With twenty points on display
And Bar was not really unhappy
At such a delightful array.

But soon disaster befell her
For the diamond Ace did not win.
Stephen was void of that minor
And trumped with a nauseous grin.
The five of clubs was to follow
And Bar came up with the King
But Betty was void in Steve's suit
Oh! What a terrible sting!

Bar seemed totally shattered
As she pencilled in her score.
What should have been a big bonus
Had turned into minus four!
With such aggressive bidding
The no-trump slam was missed:
Perhaps a new convention
Should be added to her list.

The Hand:

Betty
♠ Q 5 3
♡ 4 2
♢ Q J 10 9 8 7 6 5
♣ —

Bar
♠ K 10 8 4
♡ A Q 10 7 6
♢ 4 3
♣ K 3

Penny
♠ A J 9
♡ K J 9 8
♢ A K 2
♣ A 4 2

Steve
♠ 7 6 2
♡ 5 3
♢ —
♣ Q J 10 9 8 7 6 5

THE SCHOOLS CUP FINAL
by Alistair Flutter

In previous years this event has been sponsored by the *Daily Mail*, but this year they withdrew their sponsorship and the E.B.U. had to fund the competition on its own. Twelve teams competed in the final, most of them Sixth-Formers from Public Schools, and we were the youngest team there as well as one of the few teams from the State sector.

The first of our G.C.S.E. examinations being scheduled for the day after the final, revision adversely affected our preparation for the bridge competition. In fact we, the Chesterton 'A' team, came 11th equal! However, we enjoyed all our matches (of seven boards, against each of the other teams) and cheered the overall winners – Dulwich, closely followed by Durham, the only team to have a girl as one of its members. Here is a board from our match against them (hands rotated for convenience).

I opened 1NT as North and we reached 6◊ by South. The ♠10 was led and my partner tried the Queen from dummy which went to the King and Ace. He tried the diamond finesse and when this failed he lost a spade as well for one down.

At the other table, our opponents had been less ambitious and stopped in 5◊. West led a small club and the King held the trick. If spades were 4–2 and he lost a spade and a diamond, declarer needed two spade ruffs to make his contract without resorting to the heart finesse and so, to guard against the ◊K-x with West,

	North	Dealer: North
	♠ Q 8	Game All
	♡ A Q 7 5	
	◊ J 10 4	
	♣ K Q 9 3	
West		East
♠ J 10 5		♠ K 7 3
♡ K J 8 4 3		♡ 9 6 2
◊ K		◊ 9 5
♣ A 10 7 2		♣ J 8 6 5 4
	South	
	♠ A 9 6 4 2	
	♡ 10	
	◊ A Q 8 7 6 3 2	
	♣ —	

he made the safety play of leading the ◊A on the first round, thus preventing West from winning and leading another trump. In fact, the Ace dropped the King and declarer made all thirteen tricks when East later failed to cover the ♠Q.

This was 12 IMPs away, which did not do us much good!

UNLICENSED SYSTEMS:
THE DROOPING PASS
A system whereby a player differentiates between a poor and a reasonable hand by saying 'Pass' with 0–5 points and 'No Bid' with 6+.

CASH AND CARRIE

by Simon Ainger

Pretty enough place, Luchon (or Bagnères-de-Luchon to accord it its due title). Mountains aplenty, broad boulevards, entire population scurrying hither and thither armed with brown paper bags. One up on St Helena as far as exile goes, but one could understand why Aunt Carrie did not want to spend the rest of her natural there.

You are perplexed to find Aunt Carrie, Jeeves and B. Wooster Esquire congregated in the extremities of France? A nutshell not being to hand, I give you the gist.

My dealings in the matter of one Mrs Martha Trumpington, relict as they say – and with reference to La Trumpington, aptly say – of George Trumpington Jnr., late of New York City and late in all other respects, were becoming entangled. Jeeves, I fear, was showing no aptitude for disentanglement. It may have been due to an insufficiency of fish in the diet, but I suspect the man was sulking due to a difference of opinion with Messrs Dolby and Sons, purveyors of Glowgleam shirts. In most affairs of state, Jeeves is admirable. But no man is perfect. I cast no aspersions, I throw no stones but, on the question of sartorial elegance, he is seriously deficient. Be that as it may, the situation was such that a period of exile had a definite attraction. Do not misunderstand me, Aunt Carrie's SOS would not have fallen on deaf ears, it simply arrived at a convenient time. I have a soft spot for Aunt Carrie, mainly due to the fact that she is spouse to Sir Edgar Treadle who is both the richest and the meanest man in the realm. Uncle Edgar soaks up money like a sponge and then petrifies. Steer him towards a blind matchseller and he will stop to ask for a light. Only Aunt Carrie, who would not be averse to achieving the status of relict herself, has the knack of extracting any loot and then only by subterfuge. Indeed, if you need a transfusion in the middle of Stonehenge, my advice would be to demand Aunt Carrie as chief surgeon. The current position was that, having raided the Treadle vaults, by whatever ruse, for a period of freedom as far away from Uncle Edgar as the haul allowed, the entire treasury had vanished at the local bridge club. Not lost at the table, but stolen from her handbag. Unable to pay any bills, Aunt Carrie was marooned. An appeal to Uncle Edgar was unthinkable. Ten years of *petit point* without the option would be the lightest sentence she could expect. Hence the urgent request that I journey forth armed both with the necessary bail and Jeeves. There had been a hiccup *re* item two. I'd apprised the man of the problem and its location.

"Luchon, Jeeves. Know where it is?"

"I believe it to be a spa resort in the French Pyrenees, sir. I understand the waters there are thought to be particularly beneficial to those seeking longevity."

"Remote, is it? No chance of happening upon stray members of the family Trumpington?"

"Most unlikely, sir. I fancy they would find Harrogate more convenient."

"Excellent, Jeeves. Then we are bound for Luchon *sans* delay."

"I'm afraid not, sir. You will recall that I am on vacation next week. My presence is required by Great-Aunt Hettie in Northumberland to judge the fruit and vegetable show. You are booked into your club."

I knew that argument would be of no avail. Apart from the fact that Jeeves returned from this annual pilgrimage to northern climes a considerably richer man, owing to the hospitality of those requiring that the size of their marrows received due recognition, his Great-Aunt Hettie was, by repute, not to be crossed. Indeed, had the Duke of Wellington refereed ten rounds between her and Aunt Agatha, he would undoubtedly have come to the conclusion that it was a damned close-run thing.

"Very well, Jeeves, I shall venture forth alone. Kindly tootle off to Thos. Cook, citizen of this parish, and make the necessary arrangements and wire Aunt Carrie with the news. I shall pop down to the Drones to advise all and sundry that they will be deprived of the Wooster wisdom for the nonce."

Embarkation orders issued by T. Cook were for Thursday's boat train. On the morning of departure Jeeves brought astonishing news alongside the usual restorative.

"I will after all accompany you, sir. I have informed Great-Aunt Hettie that, due to the international crisis, I am forced to cancel my vacation. Fortunately international crises only impinge on her part of the world when the Scots become troublesome, so there was no requirement for detailed explanation."

"Top-hole, Jeeves, but enlighten me as to the nature of the crisis in question."

"It has two facets, sir. Firstly I had a communication from Lady Treadle that it would be too dangerous for you to travel alone."

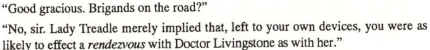

"Good gracious. Brigands on the road?"

"No, sir. Lady Treadle merely implied that, left to your own devices, you were as likely to effect a *rendezvous* with Doctor Livingstone as with her."

"Well, a raspberry for Aunt Carrie. And secondly?"

"That, sir, is an altogether more serious matter. Your valise had been disturbed and, as I was repacking it, I discovered an unsuitable item of apparel. I have abstracted it, sir, but I am concerned that other aberrations might occur without my presence."

There are times in a fellow's life when strength of character must be displayed. This was such a time. My voice was firm, my eye steely.

"I take it, Jeeves, that you are referring to a certain shirt. That being so, you can jolly well unabstract it."

Faced with such mettle, the poor man turned to jelly. The face blanched, the lip trembled.

"As you wish, sir," was all he could utter.

*****

Since the reader is by now well past the threshold of boredom, I will not rub salt into the wound by recounting our journey. Suffice it to say that for entertainment value it was on a par with Gussie Finknottle's dissertation on the lifestyle of the newt. Gloom was relieved only by the excellence of the *filet mignon*. Jeeves was less enthusiastic about the poached turbot which I required that he eat.

However, since we have broached the subject of food, I must digress to discuss the catering arrangements of the Hotel Bonne-Maison. The French have raised the business of refurbishing the inner man to an art form. Alas, this cultural excellence has not reached the Pyrenees. Those wishing to dine had to be on parade at the ungodly hour of seven pip emma precisely. One second after the last spoonful of soup left one's lips, the bowl was whipped away and replaced with the next course. And so it went on. The whole affair was over in twenty minutes flat.

"This is not on," I told Jeeves.

"No, sir."

"One can only hope that the waters are beneficial to the digestive system."

"Precisely, sir. I understand the haste is for the benefit of the *curistes* in order that they can keep to their schedules. It does, however, enable us to visit the scene of the crime. I have ascertained that there is partnership bridge at the casino starting at 8 p.m."

"You mean we play together, Jeeves?"

"That is a regrettable necessity, sir. And I fear that I must ask you to make some adjustments to your normal system of bidding."

I have to tell you that the gods rarely look kindly on B. Wooster at the card table. Offhand, I am unable to recall the last time that I won a rubber. This time, however, the Jeeves system, odd though it may seem, worked like magic. I did not get to be declarer all evening, but on the last hand I bid a grand slam which Jeeves made with no trouble. And I must say that due praise arrived with the brandy and soda.

"I must compliment you on bidding seven no-trumps, sir."

"Thank you, Jeeves. Put a franc or two in the kitty."

"Yes, sir. It also unmasked the man who purloined Lady Treadle's francs. He was sitting on your left."

"Good Lord, Jeeves. Red-nosed cove who got so upset when you made the contract?"

"The very same, sir. If you will allow me, I will elucidate."

"Elucidate away, Jeeves."

Bertie
♠ A J 10 9 4 3 2
♡ K J
♢ 5 2
♣ A Q

South	West	North	East
1◇	NB	2♣	NB
3NT	NB	7NT	All Pass

West	Red-nosed cove
♠ 5	♠ 7
♡ 10 9 8 6 3 2	♡ 7 5 4
◇ —	◇ Q J 10 8 4 3
♣ K 9 7 5 4 2	♣ J 10 8

Jeeves
♠ K Q 8 6
♡ A Q
◇ A K 9 7 6
♣ 6 3

Jeeves wrote the hand down, and I give it to you freely. The bidding perhaps needs some clarification. Jeeves opened 1◇. Under instructions from Jeeves, I was forbidden to bid spades, hearts, or no-trumps unless he had bid them first. I therefore bid 2♣. When I heard him respond 3NT, I thought, blow me, I must have another four tricks that he doesn't know about and we Woosters do not lack courage.

Jeeves began his exposition.

"The ♡10 was led. It appeared that, to make thirteen tricks, I needed the ♣K to be on my left. There was, however, no urgency to try the finesse, and I therefore played off the winning tricks in spades and hearts. During this procedure the gentleman on my right was exhibiting signs of distress. He appeared to be in great difficulty in discarding on my winners, as would a person who both held the ♣K and was guarding the diamonds. I therefore came to the conclusion that he did not hold the ♣K, and took the finesse."

"All is not clear, Jeeves," I said. "Correct me if I am wrong. Red-nosed gent appears to be holding this King, which is vital to the proceedings, which leads you to the conclusion that he is not holding it?"

"You have analysed the situation perfectly, sir. The rubicund gentleman in question had proved himself to be a very good player. If he had held the ♣K, he would have discarded without the slightest trace of inconvenience. He would have guarded the diamonds and left himself with the bare ♣K. With no clue as to its location, I might well have played for it to be in his partner's hand. I am quite certain, sir, that a gentleman who is capable of such manoeuvres is highly likely to have stolen Lady Treadle's money."

"Brilliant, Jeeves."

"Thank you, sir. The problem arises, however, as to the matter of proof. But I assume that Lady Treadle simply wishes to recover the money and not see the culprit incarcerated?"

"Good heavens no, Jeeves. The fellow looked to be past that kind of activity, but nevertheless that would be going too far."

"In that case, sir, I have a plan which might work. I shall attend to it in the morning."

✳✳✳✳✳

"I have recovered Lady Treadle's money, sir, and I have already returned it to her."

"Jeeves, you are a genius. Explain all."

"Well, sir, the gentleman under suspicion was, as you will recall, somewhat upset when I successfully made the grand slam. Indeed, he went so far as to accuse you of cheating. He seemed to be under the impression that the bidding was somewhat bizarre and that, if we were going to play in a Grand Slam, you ought to have been playing it in 7♠. This contract he would have defeated by the simple device of leading a diamond."

"What cheek. A cheat, eh? Well, I suppose I have been called worse things in my life."

"Indeed you have, sir. But not, I suspect, so profitably. I was able to tell the gentleman that you intended to pursue an action for slander. He was not impressed until I mentioned that you would be willing to settle for exactly the sum lost by Lady Treadle. I got the impression he then concluded that the game was up, and there was no further problem. Of course I also mentioned that certain expenses had to be met on top of the sum agreed."

"Including loss of income in respect of fruit and veg.?"

"Indeed, sir. Lady Treadle has also been most appreciative. She intends to include me in her will. That, of course, will only be profitable if she survives Sir Edgar. However, I gather that her reason for taking the waters here is to secure that eventuality."

"Well, Jeeves. Mission accomplished. Well done. But what now? The attractions of the place diminish rapidly hour by hour, but return at this early date seems unadvisable."

"I agree, sir, that your return to London would seem to be undesirable for the present. I have therefore taken the liberty of arranging a schedule which enables us to divert via Cap d'Antibes. It is circuitous but possible, and I fancy you would find the location more congenial."

Jeeves was a marvel. I struggled to find words to express my admiration for him. They would not come, but a great sacrifice might just possibly convey my feelings.

Luchon, I had realised, was not quite ready for Glowgleam shirts. But Cap d'Antibes would be a different story. Nevertheless.

"The Glowgleam shirt, Jeeves."

"Sir?"

"You may get rid of it."

"Thank you, sir. I have in fact already disposed of it. The chambermaid thought that it might be suitable for mopping the floor."

People and Bridge

CONFESSIONS OF A BRIDGE WIDOWER
by Dave Edmondson

Bridge, in our household, is a joint venture: my wife plays, and I look after the horses, dogs, and children. On the whole this is a very satisfactory arrangement, as it leaves me free to pursue my passion of racehorses and horse-racing. However, I suffer from one grave disability: I am an ex-bridge player who retired from competitive play at the age of forty. 'Why a disability?' you may ask. Have *you* ever suffered a post-mortem at two in the morning?

Picture the scene. After a hard day cooking, cleaning, and gardening, one retires to bed in a weary state. After a few minutes reading *Horse and Hound* one turns out the light and rapidly falls into a deep sleep.

Crash! The merry bridge player has arrived back from her congress 396 miles away. I make my first mistake. "How did you do, dear?" I open one weary eye.

"Terrible! We were only 4 VPs above average. I played like a drain. Well, I don't know that I did. How would you have played this contract?"

After three attempts I manage to get it right. Why didn't *she* think of the Scissors Coup? I should have thought it was an elementary play . . .

It's three in the morning. The inquisition is over. I wonder whether now is a good time to tell her about the chestnut gelding I purchased today?

AN EXPENSIVE MISTAKE
by John Harper

The following exciting deal occurred at the £1 Chicago table and, as you can imagine, provoked quite a heated discussion amongst members of the **Ace of Clubs**. Who do you think was the culprit?

This was the bidding:

East	South	West	North
1♠	2♡	2♠	4♡
4♠	5♡	NB	NB
5♠	6♡	NB	NB
6♠	7♡	NB	NB
Dbl	All Pass		

The result was 7♡ doubled made for 2470.

You will note that 7♠ goes only one off (unless South finds the double dummy defence of underleading his ♣A for a diamond ruff) for a loss of only 100 points (doubled, naturally). It is also interesting to note that on a non-club lead 7♠ will make, so who was at fault?

Clearly East must carry most of the blame. First, pushing his vulnerable opponents into a good slam knowing that there is freakish distribution about, is madness; second, not going to 7♠ when everyone is obviously guessing cannot be mathematically right. Even if 7♡ is going off, the risk is too great at the prevailing vulnerability, and East should know that 7♠ is almost certainly going to be cheap.

A better bid over 4♡ would have been 5◇. If East had made this bid, and South had competed to 7♡, not only would East have been in a better position to take the save but also West may have been able to bid 7♠, having no tricks in clubs or hearts himself.

North	Dealer: East
♠ —	N/S Vul.
♡ A Q 9 6	
◇ K 7 5 3	
♣ K J 10 9 8	

West	East
♠ A 10 7 4	♠ K Q 9 6 3 2
♡ J 8 5	♡ —
◇ J 10 9	◇ A Q 8 6 4 2
♣ 7 3 2	♣ Q

South
♠ J 8 5
♡ K 10 7 4 3 2
◇ —
♣ A 6 5 4

The Ace of Clubs Bridge Club

DISCARDS: DISCERNING AND DESPERATE!

by Alec Salisbury

Perhaps the first thing to be said about discards is that while they can sometimes be turned into a signal for partner, they can also be sorely inconvenient. This happens, for example,when we are forced to play a *key* card or its guard – frequently while declarer runs a long suit or draws partner's trumps. However, let's look at the positive aspects first.

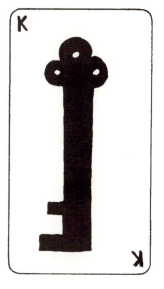

SIGNALLING WITH A DISCARD

When you signal to partner with a discard, remember that you are trying to tell him which suit to lead, not necessarily what high cards you own. Sometimes you will want a particular suit so that you can ruff declarer's winning high card, sometimes so that you can get back on lead via a winning finesse; and so on. There are many reasons for wanting to signal to partner, not only with a discard as in this discussion, but via an opening lead, or the card you play when following suit.

However, sticking to suit-preference discards, the most popular systems and the messages they convey are as follows.

McKenney (or Lavinthal) Discards

Playing McKenney discards says first and foremost that you are not interested in the suit from which you discard, but are interested in one of the other two suits. Thus, if you first discard a diamond on a spade lead, then you are interested in either clubs or hearts. Moreover, if the card discarded is *high*, then you are indicating that you would like partner to lead the *higher* of the other two suits. In other words, if you discard the ♦8 on a spade lead, you are asking partner to lead hearts. Similarly, if you discard a relatively *low* card, you are asking for the *lower* of the two other suits – namely clubs. Naturally, subsequent discards should not be interpreted as lead-directing – they are merely the disposal of unwanted cards.

The principal advantage of McKenney discards is the flexibility offered by way of choice of suit in which to discard, allied to the fact that you need never discard a high card in the suit which you want led. However, a potential disadvantage is that partner may interpret a discard as lead-directing when it is not, since we frequently need merely to discard a loser rather than a potential winner, and no signal is intended. Furthermore, a McKenney discard is usually apparent to declarer as well as partner.

Natural Discards

In this scheme of discards a *low* card suggests *lack of interest*, and a *high* card suggests *positive interest*, in the suit discarded. A high card, followed by a lower card in the same suit (a *peter*) is virtually an instruction to partner to lead that suit if at all possible.

An obvious disadvantage of natural signals is that it is not always convenient to discard a high card in the suit you want led. In practice, however, this is rarely a problem against a suit contract, when the reason for wanting the suit is usually to get, or set up, a ruff (your holding in the suit being short) or to develop, or cash, a first or second round winner (with other high cards in the same suit). Against a no-trump contract, it is far more common to discard from the suit(s) which you do not want. Moreover, unlike McKenney discards, it is usually possible to find a neutral discard, since you are in effect throwing away a card which you do not want from a suit in which you are not interested.

Of course, discard signals must not be confused with other lead-directing signals – such as indicating the suit you want returned when leading for partner to ruff, when a McKenney signal is invaluable.

Reverse Discards

To avoid the need to play a high card from a suit which you want led to you, Reverse Signals are used by some players, whereby a *high* discard is *discouraging*, and a *low* card is *encouraging*. Other variations include:

Odd–Even (even = play this suit; odd = do not play this suit).

Criss-Cross (even = play this suit; odd = play the other suit of this colour).

On balance, I think that in recent years I have detected a swing back in popularity towards the simpler, natural discards, and I certainly prefer them.

Discarding from a Sequence

When discarding an honour from a sequence, follow the same principles as for opening leads, e.g. start with the highest of a sequence. Thus the discard of a King denies the Ace and promises the Queen, and so on.

Quiz Time

Time for a couple of illustrations, based on natural discards. Try and work out the answers before looking at the solutions.

(a) You are East. South opens 2NT (20–22), raised to 3NT by North. Partner leads the ◊3. Your ten is taken by declarer's Ace. South continues with the ♣Q which wins, followed by a lower club to the King, and yet another club.

What do you discard?

Answer: You want to indicate a spade lead to partner, but are reluctant to part with the ♠9. Therefore you discourage a

North
♠ 7 5 2
♡ Q 8 6
◊ 8 4
♣ K J 10 7 3

East
♠ A Q 9 8
♡ 10 9 7 3 2
◊ 10 6
♣ 9 4

heart lead by playing the ♡2, hoping that partner will get the message and lead spades.

(b) This time you are West. Partner opens 3♣, South overcalls with 3♡, and North raises to 4♡. You lead the ♣10, declarer plays low from dummy, and partner wins with the Jack. Partner now continues with the ♣A.

Which card should you play?

```
                           North
                           ♠ A Q J 7
                           ♡ 10 5 2
                           ◊ J 8 6 4
                           ♣ K 8
                  West
                  ♠ K 10 9 6 4
                  ♡ J 7 3
                  ◊ A 9 5 3
                  ♣ 10
```

Answer: This time you do not want partner to switch, but to continue clubs in order to promote your Jack of trumps, en passant. Later the ◊A will defeat the contract! Therefore you play the ◊3, and when partner can see no profitable switch, he will continue the clubs!

DISCERNING DISCARDS

Discarding on Declarer's Long Suit

Perhaps you will excuse me for stating the obvious. Namely, that you should strive to keep winners, and discard losers, leaving partner to infer that you are interested in the suit which you have retained. There are times when these objectives are more compatible with natural discards than with McKenney.

Maintaining Length with Dummy's (or Declarer's) Long Suit

If dummy has four or more cards in a suit, try to maintain length if you can beat one of dummy's cards. For example:

```
            Dummy
            ♠ A K Q 3
West                  East
♠ J 10 6              ♠ 8 5 4 2
            South
            ♠ 9 7
```

South has three spade tricks in dummy. If East discards one of his apparently worthless cards on another suit, South will make *four* spade tricks.

```
            Dummy
            ♡ A 7 6 3 2
West                  East
♡ Q 10                ♡ J 9 5 4
            South
            ♡ K 8
```

Provided declarer has two outside entries to dummy, he can set up an extra trick via King, Ace, ruff, cross to dummy, ruff again, cross to dummy. and cash the fifth heart.

If East discards a heart, the suit can be set up for two extra winners, and only one outside entry is needed in dummy!

Maintaining Communication with Partner's Suit

If you are likely to gain the lead, try to retain at least one card in partner's suit. However, if that is unlikely, you can afford to discard all of your cards in partner's suit, so that he can obtain a full count of the suit.

Notice that when declarer shows out of a suit, you can safely discard that suit, unless trying to maintain length with dummy.

FLEMING'S GIANT CROSSWORD

(Solution on page 127)

Across

1. I respect symbolic Sun recast from out of the east. (9, 4, 6)
13. Worrisome position in which many put on years. (7)
14. There's a small enclosure in nearly all the carp. (5)
15. One who smashes burrstone, missing no fragment. (7)
16. Where to change gnats to pigs? (7–4)
17. Something bad in the blood – i.e. maculae erupt. (9)
18. Try not to let them in in disguise. (3–3)
19. Having ribs, oats, etc. being digested. (7)
20. Quiet, luxuriant year, pretentiously luxurious. (6)
23. Mr Micawber's situation? – post never properly organized. (9)
25. What you might be doing to a cold or a work of genius. (8. 3)
27. See diagram.
30. Dread of USSR's policy begins with getting USSR upset. (11)
32. Macbeth's mad about Edinburgh's capital nut-tree fruit. (5–4)
34. But not, perhaps, a Spaniel *bitch*! (6)
36. Ginger family plants mothers after a little while. (7)
37. After knocking gins back I appear in *modern Greek* city. (6)
41. Infamous Orion's out hunting. (9)
42. They make the Horn sterile, blowing about. (11)
43. Fruit of Capri? Cottage garden boasts it, too! (7)
44. Join up with chap on the way back. (5)
45. Sounds like with these you see the genuine need! (7)
46. U.S. city attorneys – very sharp ones. (12, 7)

Down

2. Is getting going again the craft of unemployed actors? (7)
3. Care is needed with rain blowing about in game on board. (9)
4. Sigh about the French transport often having bells on. (6)
5. Tending to correct Nordic tooth snaggle. (11)
6. Whosoever sits on our Throne . . . (14, 7)
7. . . . plus other scattered cushion. (9)
8. Put down time when U-boat is expected! (6)
9. I damn Lester losing form, offering less resistance. (11)
10. Sounds like berries sent Mob wild. (7)
11. Old play – rewrite (and call hooch "Foster's"). (3, 6, 3, 7)
12. Mitty sees waterfront blitzed – ended 1st Dutch War. (6, 2, 11)
21. Left little England before your very old, like the Nile. (7)
22. Dose with own mixture, having got the vapours. (7)
24. These jars sound like they might be yours! (5)
26. Japanese city, rather large, also known as ——. (5)
28. Pertaining to 'the burn'? Coarse limit needs adjusting. (11)
29. Medusa's underside – used to keep U-boats dry? (11)
31. Coming out of the blue, it —— —— out of the target! (9)
33. When low marries high – very, very high! (9)
35. What blocks passages is viscid liquid in broken arch. (7)
38. Royal Prince displaying more precipitation than usual! (7)
39. Strode, once it's ——. (6)
40. Circulated hot air used to incandesce in gas-mantles. (6)

FLEMING'S GIANT CROSSWORD

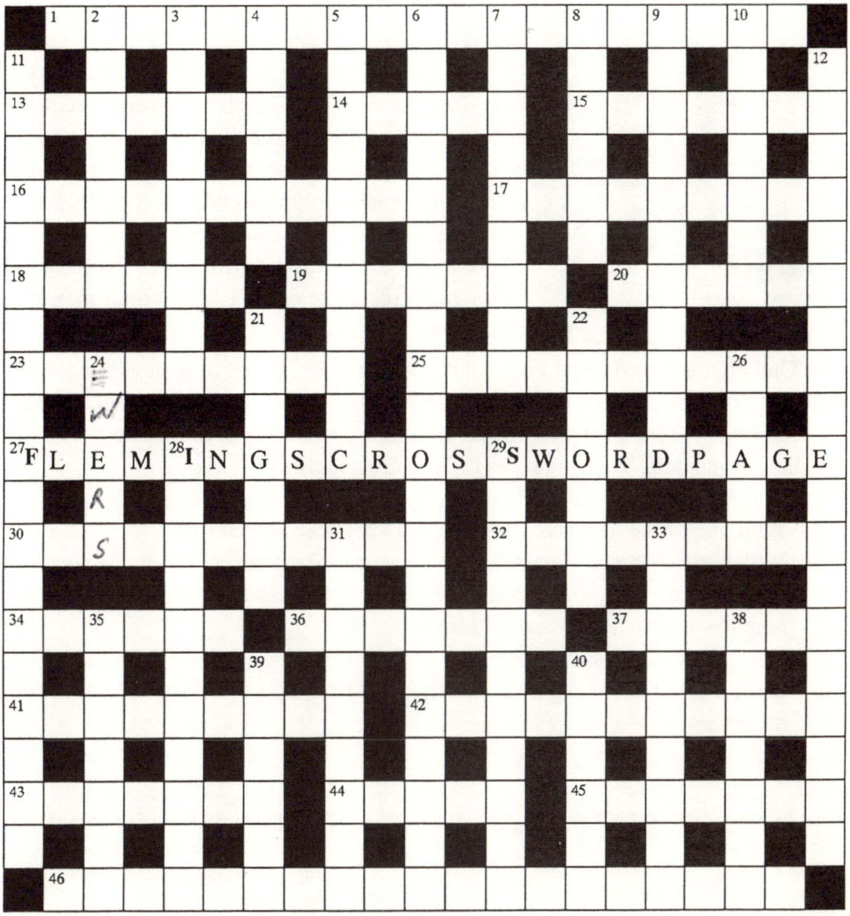

By ART

A.L. FLEMING
Rear of 12 Salisbury Road, Bromley, Kent BR2 9PY
Telephone 081-313 0350

THE NUNES GRAND SLAM FORCE

by Jack Nunes

The *Grand Slam Force* was devised by the late Ely Culbertson in 1936 and was first described by his wife Josephine, which is why it is now frequently known as *Josephine*. It is a bid of 5NT in a situation where a trump suit has been agreed and a grand slam is on if the trump holding is secure. The 5NT bid is not Josephine if it is a natural no-trump raise, or part of another slam convention, i.e. Blackwood, following a response of 4NT: this would then be an enquiry for Kings.

The Culbertson Grand Slam Force asks partner to bid seven of the agreed suit if he holds *two* of the top three trump honours, or to sign off in six of the agreed suit if holding *one* or *none* of the top three honours. The *Nunes Grand Slam Force* adds certain refinements. The responses to 5NT are as follows:

1. With two of the top three honours, bid seven in the agreed suit.
2. With one of the top three honours, bid six in the agreed suit.
3. With none of the top honours, bid a lower-ranking suit.
4. With the agreed suit a major, the response of 6♣ shows none of the top three honours and not more than four trumps.
5. A response of 6♢ shows none of the three top honours, but five trumps.
6. If the agreed suit is spades, a response of 6♡ shows six trumps, but no top honours.

Here are two examples:

West	East	West	East	
♠ A Q x x x	♠ K x x x	West	East	(a) First-round club control.
♡ A x	♡ K x x x	1♠	3♠	(b) First-round diamond control.
♢ K Q x x x	♢ A J x	4♣ (a)	4♢ (b)	(c) First-round heart control.
♣ A	♣ x x	4♡ (c)	5♡ (d)	(d) Second-round heart control
		5NT (e)	6♠ (f)	(e) Grand slam force.
		7♠ (g)		(f) One top honour.
				(g) Can count to 13 tricks!

West	East	West	East	
♠ A K x x x	♠ x x x x x	West	East	(a) First-round club control.
♡ x	♡ A x x	1♠	3♠	(b) First-round diamond control.
♢ K Q x x x	♢ A J x	4♣ (a)	4♢ (b)	(c) Second-round diamond control.
♣ A x	♣ x x	5♢ (c)	5♡ (d)	(d) First-round heart control.
		5NT (e)	6♢ (f)	(e) Grand slam force.
		7♠ (g)		(f) None of the top 3 honours, but 5 trumps.
				(g) Ten trumps between them: a good grand slam.

THE MEMORY LINGERS ON

by Pat Cotter

Pat Cotter writes for the

FINANCIAL TIMES

Some years ago I was playing *partie libre* in a bridge club on the South coast when this hand turned up. I was sitting North, partnering a Lady International. We were vulnerable and 60 below, when I dealt myself the attractive North hand below. Now slam bidding with a part-score, even among expert players, is notoriously poor, because both partners are frightened of making over-optimistic bids that may endanger the game or rubber. However, I thought fit to open with 2◇, leaving my partner to decide the height of the final contract. East overcalled with 2♠. Now, if he wants to disrupt the bidding, he should try 4♠, a bid that might prevent us from reaching a slam which we can fulfil, or goad us into one which we cannot.

	North	
	♠ 10	
	♡ Q 5	
	◇ A K Q 10 8 7	
	♣ A J 10 9	
West		East
♠ K 7 3		♠ Q J 9 8 6 5 4 2
♡ 8 7		♡ K 6
◇ 9 5 2		◇ 3
♣ K 8 7 5 2		♣ 6 4
	South	
	♠ A	
	♡ A J 10 9 4 3 2	
	◇ J 6 4	
	♣ Q 3	

South rightly cue-bid 3♠, West went 4♠, and now it was up to me. My opening two-bid was not robust, but I thought I was good enough to say 5♣. East passed, and my partner jumped to 7◇. This was somewhat ambitious, but apart from that South overlooked an important psychological factor. She should be happy to bid and make 6◇. The opponents may submit to the little slam, but it is an absolute certainty that they will sacrifice in 7♠ over 7◇, and a double might not yield an adequate return. If the opponents overcall 6◇ with 6♠, *then* she might try 7◇.

Sure enough, when this was passed round to East, he said 7♠. South should have doubled, but after a heart-searching struggle and with a muttered "I hope my partner won't mind," she bid 7NT. West doubled – I can't think why – and led the ♠K.

South won, and cashed six diamond tricks. Then she paused for thought. Knowing that a losing finesse might cost a four-figure penalty, she was wondering – so she told me afterwards – which finesse to take. That was faulty thinking. The heart finesse, if correct, lands the contract; the club finesse can provide only twelve tricks. On the diamonds South should throw two hearts and a club. Declarer took the heart finesse – it worked – but because she had thrown three hearts, there was another moment of truth to be faced. The club finesse was taken, and it won.

"Well played," I said hoarsely, and tottered out into the cool night air.

ASK THE RIGHT QUESTIONS
by Stephen Cashmore

I was standing motionless on an Intercity 125 bound from Reading to Paddington. I was standing because I had been too late to get a seat, and I was motionless because there was no room to move. My left arm was pinned by a large man wearing a donkey jacket, and my right by an elegantly dressed lady who – so my shins told me – was carrying a steel-tipped shopping basket. In front of me was a small man who jammed his head up under my chin every time the train jolted.

Unexpectedly, a hand appeared from somewhere behind me, holding a piece of paper on which was scribbled the layout shown below.

North
♠ 10 5 2
♡ 9 7
♢ A K Q 7 6 3
♣ 8 7

South
♠ A K 7
♡ A 5 4 2
♢ 9 8
♣ A 10 6 5

I started to turn around, to see who the owner of the hand was, but a voice advised: "Don't do it. You might injure someone. Just tell me how you play this hand in three no-trumps." Somebody in the carriage started violently, no doubt woken up by the unprecedented sound of a voice on a commuter train, but I relaxed as I recognized the voice of ——, one of the better players at the club. I studied the diagram curiously. The contract did not look too difficult: two spades, one heart, at least five diamonds, and the ♣A.

Of course, it would be necessary to duck the first diamond in case they were 4–1, because there was no entry to dummy except in diamonds. But wait a minute. Suppose the ♡A was knocked out early? Suddenly I realized I was missing some important information.

"What was the lead?" I asked. The small man in front of me looked vaguely surprised, and shrugged apologetically. Someone standing to his right winced as he did so.

"Three of hearts," came the reply.

Good, it looked as if I was on the right track. If the ♡A was knocked out early, then when a diamond was ducked the defence might be able to cash some hearts. My first thought was to duck the first heart, then try and concede a diamond to East. If East had a third heart, the suit would not be dangerous.

"Duck the . . ." I began, then I had a thought. Suppose, after winning a heart, the defence switched to clubs. That could be nasty. Then I had another thought. The lead was the ♡3, wasn't it? So if that was normal fourth best, then the hearts weren't dangerous anyway.

"What are their lead conventions?" I asked.

The small man looked puzzled and tried to look through the piece of paper.

"Normal. Fourth, top of nothing, that sort of thing."

"O.K., then," I said, feeling that I had cracked it. "I win the first heart in case they switch to clubs – the hearts look like they are 4–3 anyway. Then I duck a diamond in case they are 4–1. They can take three hearts and a diamond, but that's it."

Silence from the other side of the carriage, somehow disapproving.

"Were the hearts 4–3?" I asked.

"Yes."

"So I made the contract?"

"Oh yes, you made nine tricks all right."

"So I got it right, then?"

"Well . . . no." My heart sank. Why was bridge never easy? "You asked the wrong questions. You should have asked whether the hand was played at pairs, or rubber, or in a match."

Unexpectedly, the large man in the donkey jacket nodded, bumping his chin on the hat of yet another commuter standing close to the window. I decided that it must have been in response to one of his own internal thoughts.

"Why?" I enquired. "Isn't making the contract important whatever the form of bridge?"

"Ye . . . es," came the judicious reply. "Your line would be quite correct at rubber bridge, or in a match. There the safety of the contract is most important. But at pairs, overtricks are also vital. If you can score 660 and everyone else only scores 630, then that odd 30 points gives you a top score. Conversely, if you only make three no-trumps on the nose, and everyone else makes an overtrick, then you score a bottom. Even though you made the contract."

"So . . .?" I said, looking again at the diagram still held before me.

"So the odds on the diamonds being 3–2 are about 68%. Therefore it must be better not to duck a diamond, as there is a 68% chance of making ten tricks and not just nine. And there is another factor: some declarers might not know about the safety play, and bang out the top diamonds regardless. You can't afford to fall behind them, can you?"

I supposed not.

"So I asked the wrong questions," I muttered.

The big man nodded again, and I was sure the elegant lady smiled knowingly.

"Yes," said —— shortly. "Try again." The hand retreated for a moment, then returned bearing another scrap of paper.

North
♠ A 7 5
♡ K J 10 8 6
◇ A 10 7
♣ J 10

South
♠ 9 8
♡ A Q
◇ K 9 8 6 4 2
♣ A Q 3

"You are in six diamonds," said ——, "and the lead is a small heart. How do you play it?" I looked carefully at the diagram. There seemed to be one top spade, five hearts, and the ♣A. That was seven tricks, so provided I only lost one trump, the contract would be secure. If I led a low diamond and just covered whatever West played, then I could only lose one trump trick regardless of how the suit was divided. But remembering what —— had just told me, I asked: "Is this pairs, or one of your matches?"

"Pairs."

"In that case," I said, "I will play the Ace of diamonds, and assuming that no honour appears, follow it up with the King. That way I make an overtrick if the trumps are 2–2, and I still make the contract if they are 3–1."

"And if they are 4–0? In particular, if West has four trumps?"

"Then I go down. But," I added smugly, "I can't really afford the safety play in pairs, can I? It wouldn't make sense to play low to the ten of diamonds. I bet you never thought I'd even see the safety play, eh?"

My pleasure was short-lived. More waves of displeasure silence rolled across the carriage. "Surely that's right?" I asked in a small voice.

"You asked the wrong question again," said ——. The man in the donkey jacket nodded, and I glared at him suspiciously. "You should have asked," continued —— in a patient tone, "whether six diamonds was a good contract."

"Well, it's going to make more often than not."

"No, I phrased it badly. I mean, whether six diamonds is a *typical* contract. Are other players likely to be in it?"

I looked again at the diagram, and shook my head.

"Well?" demanded ——. I had forgotten that he probably could not see me.

"No," I admitted. "Most pairs will be in three no-trumps, or even five diamonds, I suppose."

"Or even four hearts," said ——. "Quite. Therefore, if you can make six diamonds, that will be a good result. Jeopardising the contract for the sake of a possible overtrick is unnecessary."

"I see. I asked the wrong question again, eh?"

"Yes. You must always ask if you are in a typical contract. If you are in a particularly good contract, you can afford to play safe. If you are in a bad contract, you may have to take chances to catch up with the field. And if you are in a typical contract, then you have to consider what the typical number of tricks is likely to be – as in the first hand I showed you."

"Oh."

"That's not the full range of preliminary questions, of course."

"Oh?"

The big man standing next to me suddenly said: "Is the lead normal?"

I gaped at him.

"If you have a lucky lead, then you might be able to play safe. If you have an unlucky lead . . ." he shook his head forebodingly " . . . then you might have your work cut out."

"I see," I said weakly.

"What is the strength of the opposition?" interposed the person standing over by the window. "Can you afford to take a chance which might work against them, but not against a stronger pair?"

"Er . . ." I said, even more weakly.

"Of course, there are all sorts of preliminary questions to ask when you are defending a hand, too," added —— from behind me.

"Buy a book?" said the elegant lady, scraping her shopping basket painfully up my legs to chest level. "I can recommend *The Pairs Game* by David Greenwood. And of course Hugh Kelsey's *Test Your Pairs Play*. I just happen to have . . ."

The train jolted, slowing down as we neared Paddington, and the small man butted me again. "Cards, please!" yelled the conductor from somewhere. "Have your cards ready!"

Another jolt. Another butt.

"Remember to ASK THE RIGHT QUESTIONS!" bellowed the man in the donkey jacket, who I now recognized as the director of a congress I had been to recently.

"I'll remember," I said dazedly.

RUBBER BRIDGE

by Margaret Armstrong

South – down eight games – being dummy
Said: "I'm bored, I would rather play rummy!"
Said her partner, quite sharp:
"I don't want to carp,
"But we'd win if your bids weren't so crummy!"

IT HAPPENED A LONG TIME AGO . . .

by Willy Brown

We had just won a Hubert Phillips match and reached the stage where there are only very strong teams left. This brought back memories of an encounter against an extremely strong team in 1964, all of twenty-seven years ago. One hand from that match is worth recalling; it was at the time written up by two of our four illustrious opponents.

Look at the deal below. When my wife Hedy and the late Daphne Francis were sitting North-South, the bidding went like this:

South	West	North	East
Daphne	Michael	Hedy	Boris
Francis	Wolach	Brown	Schapiro
1♠	2NT (a)	3♡	NB
6♡	6NT	Dbl	7♣
Dbl	All Pass		

(a) Minors.

```
                North            Dealer: South
                ♠ 8              N/S Vul.
                ♡ A 10 9 8 6 2
                ◇ 9 8 2
                ♣ J 10 5
West                         East
♠ J 2                        ♠ 10 9 7 5 4
♡ —                          ♡ J 4
◇ Q J 10 7 3                 ◇ K 6 5
♣ K Q 9 8 4 2                ♣ A 7 3
                South
                ♠ A K Q 6 3
                ♡ K Q 7 5 3
                ◇ A 4
                ♣ 6
```

The defence took four tricks: the ♠A-K were cashed, the play of the ♠Q next promoted a trump in North's hand, South also winning the ◇A. Minus 700 in the olden days. North and South admired the clever sacrifice bid, and wondered whether their husbands in the other room would find it too.

There was, however, no need to worry. Rixi Markus as South also opened 1♠, my partner George Francis (West), also bid 2NT showing the minors, but North (Tony Priday) passed. I began to wonder where all the hearts were, and decided to pass and await further developments. Rixi Markus, in her article about the hand, wrote that "it is difficult to explain why East passed", but Tony Priday in the *Sunday Telegraph* spoke of a "brilliantly judged psychic pass". South doubled the 2NT bid, my partner – thinking I might have forgotten the convention – bid 3♣ and North, with his singleton spade, decided to double. Three passes followed. The same four tricks were lost, and the contract was made: 470 to us.

North and South were not happy; I remember that it was fun to listen to their 'discussion'. Needless to say, although we gained 1170 on this board, we duly lost the match. We did, however, relish our moment of glory . . .

WHY NOT START A BRIDGE CLUB?

by Keith Jarrett

Go on – try it! It's not as hard as you might think. Two ingredients are essential: players and premises. Any small centre of population has a vast, if well hidden, pool of keen rubber bridge players. They play rubber partly because they like it and partly because, being unaware of each other's existence, they never get together to play organized bridge.

A good first step is to approach your local library – they may well let you put up a small advertisement. Some libraries even have a computer-based information service to keep residents informed about what is going on locally. Next, contact your local newspaper. Reporters are usually news-hungry and will gladly put in a small feature, particularly in a slow news week! A news item will also find its way into **BRIDGE PLUS** (call 04867 89961 if you want to extend your 'Catchment Area'). Also, do not hesitate to approach neighbourhood bridge teachers. They will probably be delighted to be told of a club suitable for their pupils. Your national bridge organization will be able to help in reaching registered teachers.

Once you have a pool of at least twelve players, start looking for premises. Most areas have a Community Centre or Village Hall which may be booked on a regular basis. Other bodies who may have rentable halls include the British Legion, Women's Institutes, the Red Cross and the Masons. Many a fine bridge club was started in the back room of a pub! The main points to look for in booking premises for a bridge club are: ample car parking; good lighting; good heating and ventilation; some sort of kitchen facilities; lavatories; security of tenure allied to reasonable rent; storage space for tables and other equipment.

When setting out your stall to attract members, make sure you attract the right people. There are many, many more weak players than 'Stars'. Certainly in the early days go for quantity rather than quality, and then set about raising the standard. If you can persuade your potential members that the club will be friendly – stick to this. Many rubber players will appear from nowhere to play the odd duplicate session *if* they do not get shouted at or derided, or have the Rule Book waved at them for every little transgression. Go easy with the Laws – in my opinion more players are driven from duplicate by 'Rule Book Phobia' than by esoteric conventions. Make a decision – is your club to be run by you or by a committee? Both styles have their pluses and minuses. Decide about smoking – 'No-smoking' is fashionable and seems to bring in the players. If you hope to play more than one session per week, include an afternoon. Rubber bridge players will flock in.

The E.B.U. and others such as A.L. Fleming are good sources of equipment. You will need a set of boards (1–32 for a start), some spare packs of cards, tables, chairs, table numbers (1–20?), table slips, personal score cards, curtain cards, and travelling score slips. Don't forget coffee, tea, sugar, cups, etc.

When planning your first duplicate session, try and estimate how many are likely to come. If numbers are small, get some Howell movement cards from the E.B.U. suitable for 3, 4, and 5 tables. With 6 tables and above, Mitchell movements can be used. Keep the movement simple and allow for late-comers to join in.

In our own case, within two years we are holding four sessions a week with a pool of over four hundred players. We often have over 20 tables – and this is in a country area in Berkshire! As I said at the beginning, go on – try it! You will meet large numbers of lovely people and have hours of hard work and fun.

But – please! Don't try it too near Cookham!

Good for a Laugh
MY LITTLE NEPHEW AND BRIDGE
by Jack Kroes

"Hello, Peter. How was the bridge lesson?"

"Hello, Uncle. Fine, thanks. Last week we had the 'Hold Up'. I held up the Ace five times, but then it was trumped."

"What about leads?"

"This is my weak spot, Uncle. I have a 25% chance of picking the right suit. But I still have to choose the right card. What is the chance that I pick the right lead?"

"The computer says nil!"

"Yesterday I held thirteen spades. I knew that if I opened with 7♠ my next opponent would bid 7NT. So I passed. The hand was passed out – everybody had 10 points. Anyway, next week we have the negative penalty double on our programme."

"You mean the negative double. That is not a penalty double, it's a take-out double."

"Then why is it not called a take-out double?"

"Because the experts discover a new kind of take-out double every day, Peter."

"But if there is a negative double, there should also be a positive double. Can a penalty double be positive, Uncle?"

"Yes, Peter, but only when you write 'plus' in your column."

"What if the contract makes?"

"In that case your partner will tell you that yours was an 'Asinine Double'!"

94

SPOT THE DIFFERENCES

by Hey

The cartoons below differ in ten details. Can you spot them? *(If not, turn to page 127 for the solution.)*

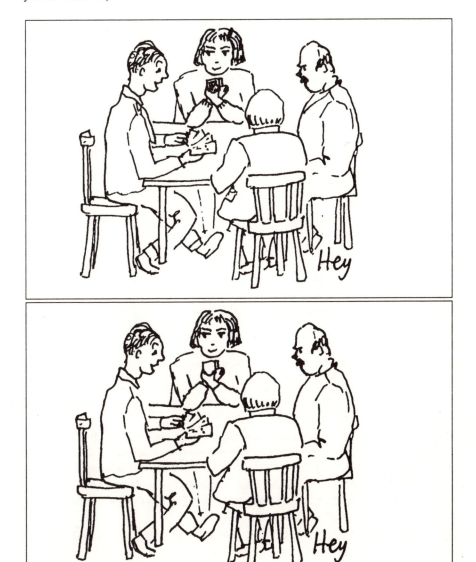

EXERCISES IN DECLARER PLAY
by Barry Rigal

In some ways it is easier to be declarer than defender when it comes to making life difficult for the other side. Dummy rarely complains at the end of the hand that you have misled him – but when you are defending, you have to bear in mind partner's sensibilities. Frequently your attempts to mislead declarer will finish up leaving you and partner with egg on your face when someone gets the wrong idea about the defence from a false card.

Anyway, the scope for giving the defence a push in the wrong direction is virtually endless. Here are some variations. Your opposition are middle-of-the- road players who use standard leads and no gadgets. In each case, you are South.

Hand 1 Pairs scoring. Dealer South	Hand 2 Pairs. Dealer South. E/W Vul.	Hand 3 Pairs. Dealer South. Game All.	Hand 4 Teams. Dealer South.
North ♠ J 5 2 ♡ J 5 3 ◇ Q 10 8 7 ♣ Q 9 4	*North* ♠ 7 5 3 ♡ Q J 10 8 7 ◇ Q 5 2 ♣ A Q	*North* ♠ J 5 3 ♡ A 10 2 ◇ A Q 9 7 3 ♣ 7 4	*North* ♠ J 9 3 ♡ K Q 7 ◇ Q 10 8 6 ♣ A J 2
South ♠ A 8 7 ♡ A K 9 ◇ K J 9 3 ♣ A K 3	*South* ♠ K J 6 ♡ A K 2 ◇ 10 6 4 3 ♣ K J 2	*South* ♠ A 6 4 ♡ Q J 3 ◇ J 10 4 ♣ A K 8 5	*South* ♠ A Q 2 ♡ J 6 5 ◇ K J 5 ♣ Q 9 6 5
You bid 2NT – 3NT, and West leads the ♡6. Any helpful extra chances when (almost inevitably) you misguess trick one?	After this bidding: 1◇　　　1♡ 1NT (15-17)　3NT West leads the ♣4. Is there time to set up the diamonds? If not, how do we maximise our chances for tricks in the spade suit?	After this bidding: 1♣　　　1◇ 1NT (15-17)　3NT West leads the ♡6. Another excellent – but not lay-down – contract. Can we improve on our good chances?	You open a weak 1NT (12-14) and partner raises to 3NT. West leads the ♠5. There are lots of tricks, but how are you going to avoid five losers?

Hand 1. This is not so much a question of deception as avoiding unnecessarily clearing up problems for the defence. If you misguess at trick one by playing small from dummy, and this goes to the ♡10 and ♡A, then West will be in no doubt that you hold the ♡K (or you would duck), and similarly East's play of the ♡10 marks you with the ♡9. Therefore he will know to switch if he has the ◇A and has to win it before getting a signal from his partner.

On the other hand, if the first trick goes ♡6, ♡J, ♡Q, and ♡K, then nothing is given away about the position of the ♡9, and West may err by pressing on with the suit when he next gets the lead.

Hand 2. Developing diamond tricks would be a long and risky process, so your best chance is to score a spade for your ninth trick. There are two issues to be borne in mind here. The first is the technical one that one cannot afford to cash the hearts off, without potentially creating squeeze and entry-blockage problems. The second is that you should be aware that East does not know whether you are trying to sneak a spade through as your ninth trick should you hold: ♠ K J 6 ♡ A K 2 ◇ K 6 4 3 ♣ J 10 2 or something similar with ♣K-J doubleton. In such a case, the right defence for him is to go in with the ♠A and press on with clubs.

You should maximise ambiguity by following with the ♣J under dummy's Queen at trick one, and then playing a spade at once. If East does not play the Ace, it is a fair inference that he does not possess it.

Hand 3. If the heart finesse is right, you should have few problems; if it is wrong, your route to nine tricks appears relatively straightforward, unless East wins the ♡K at trick one and takes it into his head to switch to a spade. While there is no law to prevent him from so doing, it behoves us to minimise the risk of this – and our best way to achieve this is to play the ♡J at trick one. Now if West has led from ♡8-6-5-4, say, and East has the ♡K-9-7, he will find it hard to read the position – for example, you could have any small doubleton.

A similar position arises when the defence lead a suit in which you have the A-J-5 in dummy and the K-10-2 in hand. Play small from dummy and win cheaply in hand, and both defenders know that the suit is dead. Play the Jack – and if the trick goes Jack, Queen, King, West at least will not know the score.

Hand 4. Obviously our play at trick one is to start by putting in the ♠9, hoping that West had led away from the ♠10 and not the King. If East plays the ♠10, we win the Queen and play the ◇K – hoping that West will do the wrong thing if he has the ◇A. We can help push him in the wrong direction by playing the ♠Q even if East does not contribute the ♠10 – trying to look like a man with doubleton ♠A-Q.

Notice that to have the best chance to beat the contract, East-West must have sophisticated signals. Imagine the layout shown opposite.

When we play a diamond at trick two, West must win and switch to the ♣7 (or 10). We play the Jack from table (two club tricks are enough for us) but East wins and sees his partner's high club. That means it is right to go back to spades. West would play a *low* club if he had, say:

♠ Q 10 6 5 ♡ 10 8 3 ◇ A 4 ♣ K 9 7 3, hoping to find partner with:

♠ 8 7 ♡ A 4 2 ◇ 9 7 3 2 ♣ Q 10 8 4, when the defence must lead and continue clubs.

North
♠ J 9 3
♡ K Q 7
◇ Q 10 8 6
♣ A J 2

West
♠ K 10 6 5 4
♡ A 8 3
◇ A 4
♣ 10 7 3

East
♠ 8 7
♡ 10 9 4 2
◇ 9 7 3 2
♣ K 8 4

South
♠ A Q 2
♡ J 6 5
◇ K J 5
♣ Q 9 6 5

by *Ian Dalziel*

RUBBER

Contract Made	Contract Defeated
♣ ◇ 20 per trick ♡ ♠ 30 per trick NT 40 first trick, 30 subsequent tricks Tricks bid score below line Overtricks score above line Game is 100 below line	Score above the line Not Vulnerable 50 per trick Vulnerable 100 per trick (You are Vulnerable when you have a game)

Rubber

First side with two games wins rubber

Two-game rubber: 700   Three-game rubber: 500

Unfinished rubber: 300 for game,   50 for part-score

Doubled Contract Made	Doubled Contract Defeated
Tricks bid score double the normal value below the line **Overtricks (above the line)** Not Vulnerable 100 per trick Vulnerable 200 per trick Insult is 50 above the line	Score above the line **Not Vulnerable** First trick 100 Subsequent tricks 200 **Vulnerable** First trick 200 Subsequent tricks 300

Redoubled Contract

Scores twice that of the doubled contract, except for "Insult" which remains at 50

Slam Contract Bonuses

Small Slam (Bid of 6):   Not Vulnerable   500   Vulnerable   750

Grand Slam (Bid of 7):   Not Vulnerable 1000   Vulnerable 1500

Honours (A K Q J 10) Bonuses

Scored by either side whether or not the contract makes

Four honours in one hand in the trump suit   100
Five honours in one hand in the trump suit   150
Four Aces in one hand at No-trump   150

DUPLICATE

Contract Made

	♣ ◇	20 per trick
For tricks made over six	♡ ♠	30 per trick
	NT	40 first trick, 30 subsequent tricks

	Part-Score	50	Game contracts are
Bonuses	Non-vulnerable Game	300	3NT, 4♡, 4♠, 5♣, 5◇
	Vulnerable Game	500	and higher

Contract Defeated

Not Vulnerable 50 per trick   Vulnerable 100 per trick

Doubled Contract Made (TIBO)

Tricks bid score twice normal value

Insult   50

Bonuses are not doubled. If the points for tricks bid after being doubled or redoubled equal 100 or more, add game bonus otherwise add 50 for part score. If slam bid, add slam bonus. (You can be doubled into game but not into slam.)

Overtricks	Not Vulnerable	100 each
	Vulnerable	200 each

Doubled Contract Defeated

Not Vulnerable

First trick	100
Second trick	200
Third trick	200
Subsequent tricks	300

Vulnerable

First trick	200
Subsequent tricks	300

Redoubled Contract

Tricks bid and made, insult, overtricks and undertricks score twice doubled value. Calculate bonuses as above.

Slam Contract

Small Slam (Bid of 6):	Not Vulnerable 500	Vulnerable 750
Grand Slam (Bid of 7):	Not Vulnerable 1000	Vulnerable 1500

Trick points and game bonus count in addition

Limitations at Aggregate

Contract defeated (smaller than slam). If defenders are Not Vulnerable their maximum score is 600 (800 if Vulnerable). Declarer scores the full loss.

Contract made (smaller than slam). If declarer is Not Vulnerable his maximum score is 800 (1000 if Vulnerable). Defenders score the full loss.

THE CASE OF THE DISAPPEARING TRICKS
by Roger Gordon

The Tuesday night duplicate in Wolfhill Prison had come to a temporary halt. The Director was at Table 2 sorting out a rather complicated dispute, which involved detailed study of the rule book, and this had resulted in the other tables having to wait for a few minutes at the end of the round. At Table 4 Anderson had been requested to perform his party piece.

"Usual stakes?" asked Anderson, shuffling the three cards.

"One cigarette," agreed the other three.

"O.K. then, if you insist. Here she is, the pretty lady."

Anderson turned up the middle card, revealing the ♠Q, then turned the card face down again. "Like all women, she should be watched very carefully." Slowly he moved the three cards around. "Easy, innit?" he said, as he turned up the right-hand card to show the Queen. "Now then, young Rafferty me lad, it's your turn . . . Find the lady!" Anderson's hands moved more rapidly, shifting the three cards from side to side. Rafferty pointed to the left-hand card, but when Anderson flipped it over the ◇2 was revealed.

"Sorry, Rafferty, you just ain't concentrating, are you?" said Anderson with mock seriousness. He repeated the process twice more, but neither Reynolds nor MacGregor had any more success than Rafferty. "Bad for me health, winning all this snout," smiled Anderson, stowing the three cigarettes in the top pocket of his shirt, then replacing the cards in their slot in the board.

"Beats me how you do it," growled an exasperated Reynolds. "Show us it again, but a little slower this time."

"Well, gentlemen, I'd love to oblige, but . . ." Anderson glanced towards Table 2, where the score on the last board was now being entered, ". . . I'm afraid it'll have to wait until another time."

In different circumstances William Anderson might have become a successful magician. As a boy, he had been fascinated by magic and had spent hours in teaching himself simple tricks. He practised on his friends, conjuring cards into their pockets or coins from behind their ears. Then one day he had discovered that it was just as easy to remove wallets from people's pockets, and had become a pickpocket instead.

Although very good at his chosen profession, Anderson was easily bored and began to take unnecessary risks to add a bit of interest to the tedious business of relieving people of their money. This proved to be his downfall, and the due process of the law brought him to Wolfhill. His ability to entertain the other prisoners with magic tricks earned him instant popularity, and also caused him to be nicknamed 'Hands'.

This was the first board of the next round, with Anderson sitting North. During the play of the hand five tricks disappeared, which tested Anderson's power of control to the limit. The bidding went as follows:

West	North	East	South
1♡ (a)	NB	4♣ (b)	NB
4♠ (c)	NB	5♣ (d)	NB
5NT (e)	NB	6NT (f)	NB
NB	Dbl	All Pass	

(a) Five-card major.
(b) Gerber.
(c) Two Aces.
(d) Gerber.
(e) Who can say?
(f) No-trumps is worth an extra 10 points.

```
                    North              Dealer: West
                    ♠ 9 4 3            Game All
                    ♡ 4 3
                    ◇ J 6 3
                    ♣ A K Q 8 6
      West                        East
      ♠ A Q J 5                   ♠ K 10
      ♡ K Q 10 8 6 5 2            ♡ A J 7
      ◇ A                         ◇ K Q 10 7 2
      ♣ 2                         ♣ J 4 3
                    South
                    ♠ 8 7 6 2
                    ♡ 9
                    ◇ 9 8 5 4
                    ♣ 10 9 7 5
```

The quality of the bidding in Wolfhill is variable, to say the least. But Anderson felt reasonably confident in doubling the final contract. He would be on lead against 6NT. If the opponents escaped to 7♡, there had been nothing in the bidding to indicate any voids, and he would still be on lead. As he waited to hear the final passes in the auction, he quickly calculated the likely score. Plus 500 was guaranteed, even if the clubs broke badly, while an even distribution would net +1400. Not bad. Not bad at all.

"Director, please!"

Anderson jumped in his seat as West's shout interrupted his thoughts. What was going on? Then he noticed. His partner had led out of turn, and the ♣10 was face up on the table! West was quick to forbid a club lead when his options were explained to him, and before you could say 'Swiss Family Robinson' had claimed thirteen tricks and a complete top.

Any thoughts of the fictional family of castaways could scarcely have been further from Anderson's mind as he put away his cards and marked the score on the travelling scoresheet. His partner mumbled a few apologies, no doubt anticipating a comment or two about leading out of turn. Suddenly, Anderson stood up, leaned on the table, and thrust his face to within an inch of his partner's face.

"I've seen some amazing things in me time, but nothing to beat that," he grated. The other three players, startled, sat frozen in immobility. Anderson reached out quickly as if to strike his partner on the side of the face, and before anyone had realised what was happening, had pulled a large steel washer from behind his partner's ear. "Just amazing . . ." he repeated, ". . . what *are* you doin' with a washer behind your ear?"

THE DENOUEMENT

by Tony Parkinson

The final match of the season in the Berks and Bucks Teams-of-Four League, Division 1, found the protagonists delicately poised. My team could either finish second or be relegated, whilst our opponents could finish third or be relegated. There was a relatively small window in the middle where neither team would go down, so after the preliminary skirmishes – 'Let's call it a draw and have a few pints down the pub' – we embarked on a disastrous first twelve boards that saw us 31 IMPs down.

The second half began much more promisingly in our room (obviously the coffee cups had been switched, and we got the stimulating ones) so we defeated a game, bid a slam, and then I came across this hand as West.

The bidding was:

North	East	South	West
NB	NB	1◇	1♠
Dbl (a)	4♠	Dbl	All Pass
(a) Negative			

North   Dealer: North
♠ 10   N/S Vul.
♡ Q 9 8 6
◇ 7 4 2
♣ K J 10 6 3

West
♠ K Q J 4 2
♡ A 4
◇ 10 8 3
♣ 8 5 2

East
♠ A 9 3
♡ J 10 7 5 3
◇ 9 6
♣ A Q 7

South
♠ 8 7 6 5
♡ K 2
◇ A K Q J 5
♣ 9 4

North dutifully led a diamond, and South cashed two diamonds and switched to the ♡K, looking to find his partner with values for his Negative Double. I won this with the ♡A and returned a heart, won by North's ♡Q. He now switched to the ♣J, and after a five-minute trance I worked out that I could not make the contract if the finesse was wrong (in which case the roof would fall in violently) so eventually I played the ♣Q and came to ten tricks for +590. Things were decidedly looking up.

Interestingly, double-dummy North-South can only defeat the contract by leading clubs initially and again when in with the ♡Q. Declarer cannot then enjoy the big

heart he has painstakingly set up in dummy. The key is of course that he needs an entry to dummy after drawing trumps, which takes four rounds – so if the clubs have been played earlier the entry has gone. However, I suspect that a club lead would not feature largely in any of the learned tomes of Bridge History for that hand.

I almost forgot – the result! There was a bit of a turnaround in the second half, so we ran out the winners by 6 IMPs, which equates to 6–4 in VPs, and another season in Division 1 for both teams.

BRIDGE IS A GAME
by Peter Mohan

Bridge is a game for the active brain,
Where trumps are hearts, when the game starts,
And the opener's call alerts us all
That the game has begun, and the game is fun.

Bridge is a game, though the contract's a strain.
When you're in one no-trump, and your hand's a dump,
Then you go down, and your partner's frown
Tells you **he** could have made it, if **he** had played it.

Bridge is a game, going off is a shame
When trumps are spades, and the contract's not made
And you bid a heart, and you're left in the cart,
And you're two off doubled, and partner's troubled.

Bridge is a game that's never the same –
Each hand you get, is different yet
From the one last night, if the bid's not right
And your sacrifice is not so nice.

Bridge is a game – your opponents maintain –
Where the points you score, matter no more
Than a bit of fun, when the evening's done;
Yet they fight like hell, to beat you as well.

Bridge is a game that's merely a name
For the playing of cards, disquieting discards,
For complex conventions, and quick interventions
And forcing cue-bids, and tactical no-bids

Bridge is a game, where you shouldn't complain
If your partner's lead is not what you need,
But the players' obsession, each duplicate session,
Is to get lots of tops, until the game stops.

Bridge is a game for the active brain,
Bridge is a game for the slightly insane,
Bridge is a game, a religion, a pain:
Bridge is the name of the game.

CONVENTIONS MADE CLOUDY
STAYMAN: a major plant found in any type of soil. Club root origin from Auction day. A hardy climber, like the Clematis, can be extended.

A knocking virus has lately caused some trouble.

Paul Bosher

BRIDGE TO FRIENDSHIP
by Bernard and Minnie Brighton

During the twenty or so years it took us to travel the UK collecting seventy-five of those magic 'Greenies', there was really little time for further activity because of that dreadful four-letter word: WORK. On retirement, therefore, it was quite natural that we should devote more time to the real purpose of life on this planet – Bridge – in all its wider aspects: computing, administration, teaching, running events and, above all, widening our circle of friends to include Europe.

The first contact came with a visit to Sheffield by ten players from Minsk – in Russia. Although this was an unforeseen contact, it turned out to be the start of something big and very, very exciting. Next, up came an invitation to go to Spain as resident TDs during March. Then, without pause, we were off to Moscow, Leningrad and Minsk for ten days. This was followed by a trip to Hirtshalls in Denmark then, with a few new European friends, a visit was made to Budapest for a Ladies' international event. Thirteen players then arrived in Sheffield from our twin city of Bochum in Germany, and a return visit planned for the next year. We thought we were in for a little rest, but hardly had there been time to unpack than Minsk decided to hold their first international event, and we were off again for another ten days.

Experience had shown that there was little time for really serious bridge and, after all, regular partnerships should not be so discourteous as to actually try and *win* every competition in sight! On the contrary, these were all happy occasions where ordinary club players were to form firm and lasting friendships – and, as far as we were concerned, to enjoy the most marvellous Russian hospitality. From the moment of being specially met at the airport to the last tearful parting, we were escorted everywhere – the Red Square in Moscow, the Winter and the Summer Palaces in Leningrad, the Opera – rubber bridge (using the Strong Vodka Pass system) filling the gaps in our very full timetable.

Bridge is seen as the means of creating greater friendship and co-operation. The Russians perceive Europe as becoming smaller and the game of bridge leading the way, by working towards a single European Bridge Controlling Body with common Local Points, agreed systems, rules, and ethical standards. A good start has been made with English being *the* European bridge language. We certainly became infected with the Russians' enthusiasm and can vouch for the fact that a bridge exchange may well turn into the journey of a lifetime.

BRIDGE TRIVIA QUIZ
by Chris Kinloch

1. Which famous bridge player and author of many books including *Winning Bridge Made Easy* died on 3rd April 1991 at the age of 90?
2. Who was a member of the winning Gold Cup team in 1936 and went on to pursue a successful career in politics, including a term as a Cabinet minister?
3. Who wrote about a Rueful Rabbit, a Hideous Hog, and a Secretary Bird, amongst others?
4. What was the nationality of the inventor of the Precision Club System?

5. What do the terms DOPI and ROPI mean?
6. To what does the Acol System owe its name?
7. Which American bridge player once played opposite the Marx Brothers in *Animal Crackers*?
8. Who formulated the Blue Club System?

9. Which suit was key in *The Story of an Accusation*?
10. Who were the members of the famous 'Blue Team', sixteen times winners of the World Teams Championship?
11. Who wrote *A Bridge Too Far*?
12. Where would you find 'The Bridge of Sighs'? (*The answer is emphatically NOT at your local club! —Ed.*)

(*Solutions on page 127.*)

ANOTHER NEAR MISS

by Arthur Perelman

Recently, our team of four experienced a slight hiccup. We lost a match in our local league. We were leading by a few IMPs until the last two hands. Then, at the end, things went wrong. I was sitting North and this was the penultimate hand.

Partner raised my 1♠ opening bid to 3♠ and I bid the game. After a club lead, I drew trumps and set about the hearts. Unfortunately, I took the wrong view and lost to the ♡Q. Our opponents then proceeded to take three diamond tricks.

"Sorry, partner," I said. "I was unlucky with the hearts. Whenever I have a two-way finesse, I always play for the Queen to be over the Jack."

"Absolutely pathetic!" was his reply.

"What do you mean?" I asked.

```
                    Me
                    ♠ A K 6 5 4
                    ♡ A 10 4
                    ◊ Q 4 2
                    ♣ A 6
West                             East
♠ 8 7                            ♠ Q
♡ 9 7 2                          ♡ Q 8 6 5
◊ K J 8                          ◊ A 10 9 3
♣ 10 9 8 7 3                     ♣ Q J 5 2
                    South
                    ♠ J 10 9 3 2
                    ♡ K J 3
                    ◊ 7 6 5
                    ♣ K 4
```

"Whenever you see a two-way finesse, you start thinking about your stupid rule of Queen over Jack. Instead, you should be thinking about how to endplay the opponents. A child of six could make that contract. Just draw trumps and eliminate the clubs. Then, get off lead with a diamond. The worst that the opponents can do is to take three diamond tricks. After that, anything they lead will give you your tenth trick."

There was a pregnant silence, as we picked up our cards for the last hand of the match.

This was the bidding:

East	South	West	North
2◊ (a)	NB	2NT (b)	NB
3NT	All Pass		

(a) Acol
(b) Negative

```
                    Me
                    ♠ 10 9 8 5 4
                    ♡ A J 10 8 2
                    ◊ 9 2
                    ♣ K
West                             East
♠ 7 6                            ♠ K 3
♡ K 7 6 5 4                      ♡ —
◊ J 3                            ◊ A K 10 8 7 6 5 4
♣ Q 8 7 6                        ♣ A J 5
                    South
                    ♠ A Q J 2
                    ♡ Q 9 3
                    ◊ Q
                    ♣ 10 9 4 3 2
```

After our opponents' eccentric bidding, I was on lead. I estimated that, after our disaster on the previous hand, the two teams were about level. If so, it would all hinge on this last hand and the outcome was likely to depend on my opening lead.

'Well, here goes,' I thought to myself, as I led the ♡J. I was pleased to see East looking distinctly worried, as he tabled his hand. "I hope you have a heart stop, partner," he said.

My partner played his ♡Q and West won with the King. She then proceeded to win all the remaining tricks – eight diamonds and four clubs. My ♣K dropped on the first round of the suit and my partner had, by then, discarded his club stop.

I turned to East. "You were jolly lucky there," I said. "If I had happened to lead my ♠10 and my partner had switched to his ♡Q, declarer would have been in real trouble. I don't know whether we would make the first ten tricks or only nine. Declarer can keep us to nine tricks, if she does not play her ♡K. But, surely, she would try for her only chance to get home. Then, she would only make three tricks."

My partner interrupted. "It would be better if you did not aim quite so high. I agree that six down would be an excellent result for us. But, quite frankly, I would be satisfied with two down. From the bidding, you should infer that East is gambling and that there is a good chance of there being a hole in his bucket – provided we can find it in time. The best policy is the same as that against a gambling 3NT opening bid. If you have an Ace, lead it. A look at dummy and at partner's reaction to your lead may tell you how to carry on. This applies particularly because you are sitting *under* the strong hand: a lead through the strong dummy could turn out to be lethal – as in this case.

"If you had led the ♡A, I would not have known whether you had the King as well. But what I could have seen very clearly was that a switch to spades would definitely have been good for us. Consequently, I would have discouraged a heart continuation by playing my three on your Ace. Once you know that I don't like hearts, the only possible switch is spades and we would take the next five tricks. Even if we had muddled the spades and blocked the suit, we would still have defeated the contract. Even one off is better that four overtricks!"

We went across to the other table to score up. I found that my estimate of the state of the match had been surprisingly accurate. Before the last two hands, we had been 7 IMPs up. On these two hands, the results at the other table had been, respectively, 3♠ by North-South, making ten tricks, and 5◊ by East-West, making eleven tricks. Instead of two good positive swings, we had lost 6 IMPs on the first board and 3 IMPs on the second. We had lost the match by 2 IMPs.

"Oh dear," I exclaimed. "I seem to have lost the match on those last two hands."

"Never mind," said my partner. "Perhaps we can persuade our opponents to play 22-board matches in future."

Our other pair laughed, and I managed a sickly smile.

ALAS IN WONDERLAND
by Ron Klinger

One week before

The doorbell. Arthur opened the door and Conrad did a jig into the living room.

"You won't believe this." Conrad threw a package to Arthur. "Go on, open it."

Arthur carefully slit the top of the packet. Out slid a copy of an imminent Simultaneous Pairs' hands, the glossy cover, the advertisements, all the deals with analyses and scores. Arthur gasped, "Where . . . how did you get this?"

"Our club director was locking the hand records into the safe. He didn't notice one copy slip behind the cupboard but I did. When the session was over and everyone had left, I just retrieved it. What a bonanza."

"But what are we going to do?"

"Very simple. You and I are going to get the biggest score ever seen in this tournament. Firstly, we cancel our entry at our club, and I'll enter us at a club where virtually no-one knows us. Next, you and I are going to go through each of the hands and produce auctions to achieve the best possible score. We'll take into account all the probable opposition actions and see how best we can counter them. This is just amazing. Let's start right away."

They sat down and spread out the handbook at Hand 1.

"If I can't book a North-South seat," said Conrad, "we'll make sure we get there early to take the North-South positions. I've already had a glance through the hands, and the opportunities for North-South are better than for East-West. See what the commentary says about this deal. East-West have an easy save in 5♣ and if that goes for only one off we get 100, and that scores just above average, 56/100. Even 300 is worth only 69. We need to be able to buy the hand in 4♡ and stop them saving. Any ideas?"

```
                North           Dealer: North
                ♠ A 10 9 7 3    Love All
                ♡ 10 8 7 5 3
                ◇ Q 4
                ♣ 10
West                            East
♠ J 8                           ♠ K Q 4 2
♡ K 9                           ♡ —
◇ K J 9 2                       ◇ 10 8 7 6 5
♣ A Q 7 6 4                     ♣ J 5 3 2
                South
                ♠ 6 5
                ♡ A Q J 6 4 2
                ◇ A 3
                ♣ K 9 8
```

"It's no good making any distributional bids or show a strong fit in hearts. That will goad them into the sacrifice. We need to keep the heart fit concealed."

"How about this? I'll go North, you go South. After two passes let's say you open 1NT. Not too far-fetched in third seat, and you can always say you wanted to protect

108

your ♣K. West is likely to pass and if so, I'll just Stayman, and we'll bid to 4♡ that way. If West does come in, I'll manufacture some bid, you still don't show your hearts. Just stick with the no-trumps. I'll take it out into 4♣ or 4◊, forcing you to pick a major. It will sound as though you have no major and are reluctantly forced into accepting one."

"OK, sounds fine to me."

On the night

West	North	East	South	
	Conrad		Arthur	(a) Alerted by Arthur. "Not sure. Could
	NB	NB	1NT	be diamonds or could be asking for a major."
2♣	2◊ (a)	3♣	3NT	(b) Again alerted by Arthur. "Sounds
NB	4◊ (b)	Dbl	4♡	like diamonds, but I'm really not
NB	NB	NB		sure." 'Nice touch,' thought Conrad.

West led a low club (!) to East's Jack and South's King. Arthur returned the ♣8, pitching a diamond from dummy when West played low. After the ◊A and a diamond ruff, a heart was led to the Ace. South ruffed his last club and, secure for eleven tricks, he exited with a heart to West's King. Neither Conrad nor Arthur could believe their good fortune when West led a diamond, giving Arthur a ruff-and-discard, and allowing the spade loser to disappear.

Arthur and Conrad could scarcely contain themselves as they wrote in plus 480, 96/100.

One week before

"OK, what about Board 2?" said Arthur, turning the page.

They both studied the diagram and the expert analysis.

"Well, here it suggests you protect with 1NT when 1♠ is passed to you, but that allows East to get out into 2♡. You could just pass out 1♠."

"Firstly, if East decides to start with 1NT, we will pass that out. You lead a diamond. I'll win and switch to the ♠Q. We can take four spades and five diamonds before East gets in. That will give us 150 and 95/100. That's easy. Now, I don't know about passing out 1♠. We need to take our diamond winners to stop him pitching

	North	Dealer: East
	♠ Q J 2	N/S Vul.
	♡ J 7 3 2	
	◊ A K 3	
	♣ J 8 5	

West		East
♠ 7		♠ K 9 5 4 3
♡ 10 8 5 4		♡ A K 9 6
◊ 7 6 4		◊ Q 10
♣ K Q 7 3 2		♣ A 9

	South	
	♠ A 10 8 6	
	♡ Q	
	◊ J 9 8 5 2	
	♣ 10 6 4	

one on the third club, but then he can play three rounds of clubs later and ruff a diamond. The ♡A is five tricks, and then the ♡K ruffed by you endplays you into giving him a sixth trick. Plus 50 is worth only 69/100."

"You could double 1♠ and I could pass it out for plus 100. That gives us 82."

"Yes, but West might redouble and then they might find 2♡. No, I've got a better idea. It's a bit risky, but worth the chance. You overcall 1♠ with 2◊ . . ."

"On that heap of rubbish, vulnerable against not? You know I'd never do that."

"I know that, but no-one else does. Anyway, if anyone does question it, our stock answer will be that we decided to take all sorts of chances just to try to create a big score. Don't worry, just bid 2◊. I can genuinely bid 2NT, and you can leave it in. Now East could find the ♣A lead, but I bet he leads a low spade. I suppose East could cash the ♡A, switch to clubs, and have West switch back to hearts later. They could take the first nine tricks in no-trumps, just as we could in defence. I think we should gamble on the standard spade lead. We could even get lucky and have East lead a low heart. OK?"

"Fine."

On the night

West	North	East	South
	Conrad		Arthur
		1♠	2◊
NB	2NT	All Pass	

East led the expected spade and Conrad won with the Queen and continued the spades. Later he cashed the ◊A, ◊K, and when the Queen conveniently dropped, they had nine tricks.

"Plus 150, 95/100, you boys are going quite well," observed East. "Just a bit lucky," said Conrad, noticing Arthur pale slightly.

One week before

And so the partners planned on, board by board, with Arthur making notes as they went. Some of the boards were subtle, others outlandish. On Board 21 they had an argument.

```
              North         Dealer: North
              ♠ K J 7 3     N/S Vul.
              ♡ K J 3 2
              ◊ 6 4
              ♣ J 8 3
West                        East
♠ 6                         ♠ 5 2
♡ 8                         ♡ A 5 4
◊ A K J 10 3                ◊ Q 8 7 5 2
♣ A K Q 10 7 6              ♣ 9 5 2
              South
              ♠ A Q 10 9 8 4
              ♡ Q 10 9 7 6
              ◊ 9
              ♣ 4
```

"Well," said Arthur, "East-West are cold for 6♣ or 6◊. What is the best we can do to keep them out of their slam?"

"Hard to keep quiet whatever we do. Our best shot if they bid the slam is to save, and it must be in hearts. If we play in spades, they could find a heart ruff for three down and minus 800. That gives us only 52/100. If we play in 6♡, they can get only 500 and at least we'll get 63/100 then."

"But how can we reasonably play in hearts? If I start with 1♠, how can you not support my spades?"

"I guess I'll have to start the bidding. Why don't I psyche 1♡?"

"Are you kidding? 1♡ on that lot, first in hand at unfavourable vulnerability! How can you justify that? And how will you reconcile that with the other actions we've decided on?"

"Such as?"

"Such as my pass as dealer, at Love All, on Board 11 with 8 points or my pass on Board 18, second-in-hand, with 9 points. How can you explain opening here at adverse and not opening those?"

"Will you quit worrying? No one is going to look at your other passes. Why should they bother? We do not have to explain any of these passes, only my opening. And that can be explained as just a psyche. So we are vulnerable. So what? All the better to psyche since no-one will believe I'm doing it."

On the night

West	North	East	South	
	Conrad		Arthur	As expected, West could not be
	1♡	NB	4NT	contained and Arthur bid 6♡ when
5NT	NB	6◊	6♡	East produced 6◊ ('I can always say I
7◊	Dbl	All Pass		was not sure whose hand it was and so

bid 6♡ just in case,' he thought.)

When West came to their rescue with that 7◊ bid, Conrad doubled with glee. ('If my partner could bid 4NT, they could surely not make it and I felt I had to double to warn partner not to go on. After all, I had almost psyched. Take the plus was my thinking. Yes, that's how I'll explain it,' thought Conrad.)

South led the ♠A, not too surprisingly (any other suit allows the grand slam to make). Plus 100 (or 100/100) to North/ South.

One week before

The two artful conmen finished going through the hands and Arthur had made copious notes covering as many eventualities as they could imagine. "All right," he said. "Let's call it a night, but we can get together the night before the event and go through these all again. I could do with a dress rehearsal. And let me know where we are playing as soon as possible, will you."

He showed Conrad out.

✱✱✱✱✱

What happened to Conrad and Arthur on the actual night? Who can tell? After all, they are mere figments of the author's imagination. They do not exist in real life.

The only resemblances the story bears to real life are in the enormous scores now needed to do well in large simultaneous events and the fact that the hands used, for fictional purposes only, were taken from an actual competition.

A NARROW VICTORY

by Bernard Magee

My team (from Bristol University) was desperately in need of some luck. We were 30 IMPs down, playing badly, with only eight boards to go. Our prayers and thoughts must have floated together as two game-swings came our way and then this – the penultimate board. I was sitting West.

			North	Dealer South
			♠ Q J 10 7 4 3	N/S Vul.
			♡ J 6 3	
			◊ —	
			♣ K 8 7 6	

South	West	North	East
3◊	3♡	3♠	4♡
NB	NB	NB	

North led the ♠Q and South reasoned that North, holding six spades to the Queen (he could not have the ♠K, or he would have led it) had to have a diamond void in order to introduce a new suit in the auction. So, after taking the ♠A, he played the ◊9 (so as to deny a good club holding). North duly ruffed, and returned another spade.

```
         Me                      East
         ♠ K 9                   ♠ 8 6 2
         ♡ A K Q 7 4             ♡ 10 9 2
         ◊ 10 4 3               ◊ A J 7
         ♣ A 10 9               ♣ Q 5 3 2
                 South
                 ♠ A 5
                 ♡ 8 5
                 ◊ K Q 9 8 6 5 2
                 ♣ J 4
```

I took this and drew trumps in two rounds. Then the ◊A and a spade ruff left the following position:

Now I knew that North held the ♣K, since South would have 12 points with it and would not pre-empt in diamonds. I also knew that South could not have more than two clubs, his shape being probably 2–2–7–2. So I led ♣A and another club.

```
                 ♠ 10 7
                 ♡ —
                 ◊ —
                 ♣ K 8 7 6
         ♠ —              ♠ —
         ♡ Q 7            ♡ 10
         ◊ 10             ◊ J
         ♣ A 10 9         ♣ Q 5 3 2
                 ♠ —
                 ♡ —
                 ◊ K Q 9 8
                 ♣ J 4
```

North was helpless. Going up with the King would give declarer two club tricks (the ♡10 being the necessary entry). Ducking would

mean that a diamond would endplay South. Whatever North did, the contract was safe: +420 to our side.

At the other table, North ended in 3♠ undoubled. East led a heart, which kills the defence, and allowed declarer eight tricks for minus 100. Thus we gained 8 more IMPs to scrape home by 1 IMP!

PARTNERS

by Ruth Watson

I run a Marriage Bureau. Well, perhaps I exaggerate. It is more of a dating service than a marriage bureau. You see, I teach bridge, and run novice duplicate sessions to introduce my pupils and rubber bridge players to the fun and rules of competition bridge. Most of my problems do not occur at the class or while we are playing bridge, but on the telephone beforehand.

"Ruth, my husband is away this week, but I want to come to play bridge as usual." *"Of course, you will always have a partner because if there is no one else to partner you I stand by each week."* "Yes, but . . ." *"Well?"* "I couldn't play with H . . ." *"Oh! Why not?"* "He's too aggressive; and I can't play with K . . ." *"Oh! Why not?"* "Her son and my daughter live next door to each other, and since his cat dug up her seedlings five years ago the families haven't spoken to each other." *"Oh, well, do come along and I'm sure I'll fix you up!"*

"Ruth, we have arranged a four to play at home so that my mother can have a game (she's 86 and can't get out to the club), but now Mrs X has called off. Can you suggest a fourth?" *"How about Mrs Z?"* "She's already playing." *"Mrs W?"* "I've tried her." *"Mrs Y?"* "Of course, why didn't I think of her!"

"Ruth, I've got a friend who has got a friend who wants to learn bridge. Can you teach her?" *"Sorry, I can't, but I've got a friend who is doing some home teaching and she may be able to fit your friend into that group."*

"Ruth, I really do find that my partner is making more mistakes than ever. How can I make a change without hurting him?" *"How about coming along to the main club session on a Thursday instead of playing at the novice sessions? I'm sure you are ready for something more challenging now."*

"Ruth, the boys at my school are getting very keen, but they need some sterner opposition before they enter the schools' pairs event." *"Contact Mrs Jones, she organises the bridge at the Girls High School, and you can arrange a match between your pupils."*

"Ruth, my husband and I love coming to the bridge sessions, but we argue all the time. Is he right or am I?" *"Why don't you ask the Smiths if they will split up occasionally? You could play with Mrs Smith and your husband with Mr Smith. They never stop arguing either."*

Perhaps my Marriage Bureau has a bit of Marriage Guidance thrown in.

JOIN THE DOTS
by Hey

Join the dots in numerical order to find an object with a familiar name! *(Solution on page 127.)*

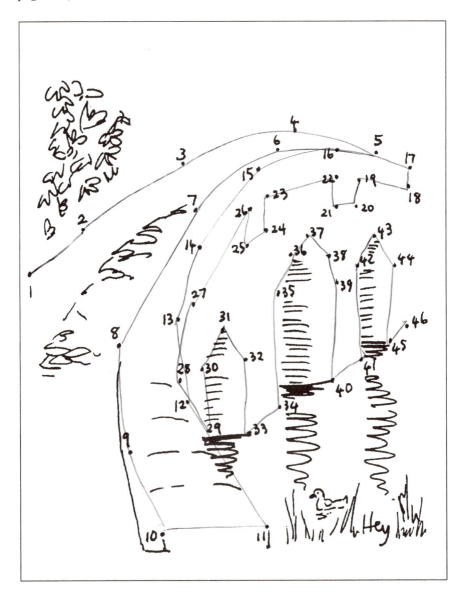

114

CLEVELAND CLUB CONVENTIONS

by David Lawton

Our club is justifiably proud of its leaders in bridge fashion. We firmly believe the Baron System was named to honour our own John Baron. We also boast the pair who devised *The Blue Seance*, a variant of the Blue Club. In their system (if you'll pardon the word) not a single bid means what it says, resulting in the table being thumped every time the practitioners mumble their incantations. Let's say they are sitting North-South against you. The auction sounds like this:

North: "One Club."

South: *Thump*!

East: "What does that mean, please?"

South: "It could be a balanced 7 to 19 , or 5 to 38 points with 3 hearts and 2 spades."

East: "Rubbish. I reserve my rights. No bid."

(South is a genial fellow; he shrugs amiably. North was as startled as you were by the explanation; he plucks at his beard and ponders.)

South: "One diamond."

North: *Thump!*

West: "What does 'one diamond' mean?"

North: "It could be 2 to 15 points or a void in spades and four hearts to the Jack."

(South was jerked bolt upright by North's exposition. He takes a swig from his can of Foster's.)

North: "One heart."

South: *Thump!*

(The bridge table is now an oujia board. Ashtrays jump nervously and two pens roll off onto the floor. The spirits are restless, especially the whisky in your glass.)

East: "Any point in asking what that bid meant?"

South: "Not a lot. I'm not sure myself. Anyway, I'm responding one spade."

North: *Thump!*

Crescendo! South's beer can topples over, soaking your convention card. Enough is enough. Without further questions, you let North and South carry on bidding and thumping merrily. It sounds like the Last Night at the Proms. At last, breathless and exhausted, they settle on an implausible final contract – just as the Director calls, "Move for the next round, please."

When everybody else has gone home, you look at that board. Every other pair bid 1NT raised to 3NT. We do have fun at the Cleveland Club.

THE EXCITEMENT OF BRIDGE

by Anna Gudge

I was born in December 1946 in London and we moved to Suffolk when I was 6-months old. I was educated at a local convent boarding-school and then went on to college to take a National Diploma in Business Studies.

I married shortly after leaving college and went out to work for five years before daughter one, Vicki, was born. She was followed in due course by daughter two, Catherine – now they are 18 and 16. Once Catherine started school, it was back to work and I undertook a variety of jobs for some years. It was during this time that I learned to play bridge – the sort that says 'open 1NT on 16-18' but neglects to tell you that you should also have a balanced hand, so you obediently open 1NT with a 6–5–1–1 shape and wonder what went wrong!

After a while my husband and I separated, and I moved house and started looking for something I could do from home, since I needed to be around for the children. My bridge had improved by that time and I had joined the E.B.U. It was in *English Bridge* that I saw an advertisement for a new B.B.L. Secretary. From the tone of the ad, it sounded as if the job had to do with bridge, even though at the time I did not have the faintest idea what the B.B.L. was. However, I applied and got the job. When I started, it was about one and a half days a week and the office equipment consisted of a battered filing cabinet and a typewriter in small pieces. It's a very different story today . . .

John and Anna Gudge

In 1989 I moved house again, to my present home, and re-married on New Year's Eve that year. My husband John works with me, and the whole operation is carried on from our dining room.

Although the British Bridge League takes up most of our time, we also do quite a lot of work for the World Federation and the European Bridge League.

This involves travelling to most of the major championships, and we consider ourselves very fortunate to be able to get to places like Finland, Venice, and Athens to name but a few.

The most exciting trip is taking place this autumn, when we are engaged to run the Press Room at the World Championships in Japan. It is a very full, exciting, and occasionally frustrating life style, but I would hate to change it. We love it!

KITCHEN BRIDGE
by Sheila Caves

The pleasure of a game of bridge among friends is heightened by sharing a meal. There is no need to produce a seven-course *cordon bleu* dinner: a light repast is all that's needed to enhance an evening together. Why not try the two recipes below?

Savoury Pie

This is ideal for using leftovers. Quantities are variable and sufficient for two flans. *N.B.* Use only Campbell's Condensed Soup, other soups change the flavour.

Pastry
12 oz. plain flour
½ teasp. salt
6 oz. margarine or cooking fat
Water to mix

Make the pastry in the usual way and line two 8" flan dishes. Bake blind for 15 minutes until just set. Gas Mark 7 (450°F – 230°C).

Filling
3-4 rashers of bacon (preferably smoked)
1 large onion
A handful of frozen peas, carrots, or
*   peppers, or a mixture of all three*
12 oz. (approx.) cooked chicken
8 oz. (approx.) mushrooms
1 tin of Campbell's Condensed Chicken
*   Soup (DO NOT DILUTE)*
Salt and pepper
Tomato for garnish

Roughly chop the bacon and lightly fry for 2-3 minutes in butter and/or oil. Finely chop the onion, add to the bacon, and cook until soft. Roughly chop the mushrooms, add to the mixture, and cook for a further 2-3 minutes. Add the peas and finely-chopped carrots and peppers. Remove from heat and mix in the soup and cooked chicken. Season with salt and pepper.

Divide equally between the flan cases, return to oven (Gas Mark 4-5 – 350-375°F – 180-190°C) for 20 minutes. Garnish with sliced tomatoes and serve.

Pineapple Surprise

1 large packet of crushed digestive biscuits
2-3 cups of icing sugar
1 tin of crushed pineapple
2 eggs
Half cup of margarine of butter
Half pint of double cream, whipped
Kirsch (optional)

Put half the biscuits into a glass serving-dish. Cream the fat, eggs and icing sugar until soft and spread over the biscuits. Drain the juice from the pineapple. Add the pineapple, with a dash of kirsch, to the whipped cream and mix well. Spread over the icing-sugar mix. Top the remainder of the biscuits. Chill in the refrigerator for at least 8 hours before serving.

SIMPLE OVERCALLS IN THE IMMEDIATE POSITION

by Albert Dorrington

Overcalling is an aspect of the game that books do not treat at all well. The point-count system used by opener and his partner to value their hands does not apply to the other two hands, and writers use phrases such as 'a good suit' and 'playing strength', descriptions which in themselves do not mean a lot to most players. When overcalling or responding to an overcall, I usually find myself resorting to the 'hope-for-the-best' version of Acol. There is a need for both the potential overcaller and his partner to be able to make quantitative assessments of their hands, and also a need to give the subsequent bidding some precision. I would like to suggest the following as a basis for discussion.

Only the simple suit-overcall made by the player sitting on the left of the opening bidder is under consideration. This player is referred to as the Immediate Overcaller (IO) and the suit is bid at the lowest possible level.

The IO has two tests to use and both must be satisfied before making an overcall.

(1) Suit-Quality Test

Length of suit bid +.Honours in suit = (at least) the number of tricks bid. At least five cards in the suit are needed and the Jack and the 10 are counted as honours only if a higher honour in the suit is held. I have only seen this brilliant idea mentioned in Klinger's *Acol Flipper.*

(2) Playing-Trick Test

Count the number of playing tricks in the hand, and use the *Rule of Two and Three.* This rule states that if you are vulnerable, you can bid two tricks light, and if you are non-vulnerable, you can bid three tricks light. Use the following method for counting tricks:

A = 1
A-K = 2
K = 0.5 (*not* for singleton K)
Q = 0.5 (if there is a higher honour in the suit)
J = 0.5 (if there is a higher honour in the suit)
10 = 0.5 (if there are *two* other honours in the suit)
Half trick for a fourth card in the suit.
One trick for each card more than four in a suit.

The strength of the hands for which a simple overcall can be made varies from four playing tricks (at the one-level, non-vulnerable) to seven tricks.

118

Satisfying the Tests

Let us see those tests in use on two hands. On both hands, suppose the player on your right opened the bidding with 1♠; you are vulnerable and considering a bid of 2♡.

Hand 1
♠ 9 7
♡ A J 9 8 6 2
◇ A K 5
♣ 7 5

The Suit-Quality Test is satisfied: *6 hearts + 2 honours = 8*, and 2♡ is eight tricks.

The Playing-Trick Test is satisfied too: the hand is worth six tricks. The *Rule of Two and Three* tells you that, when vulnerable, you can bid two light; the counted six tricks are two less than the eight tricks of the 2♡ bid. Therefore, make a call of 2♡ on the hand over the opening bid of 1♠.

Hand 2
♠ A 5 2
♡ K J 8 5 2
◇ K J 7
♣ Q 6

Dealer, on your right, has once more opened with 1♠. The Suit-Quality Test is not satisfied: *5 cards + 2 honours = 7*, i.e. not the eight required.

Therefore, do not overcall with 2♡ on this hand; the heart suit is not good enough.

Both tests must be satisfied to justify a bid, so it is not necessary to count the tricks. But, as a matter of interest, this hand also fails the Playing-Trick Test. The count gives 4.5 tricks, less than the minimum six required.

Note that if, instead of bidding 1♠, RHO had bid 1♣ or 1◇, and if you were non-vulnerable, you could have bid 1♡ on *Hand 2*. The Suit-Quality Test is satisfied because 1♡ is seven tricks. *The Rule of Two and Three* says that you can bid three tricks light if you are non-vulnerable, i.e. four playing tricks is enough at the one-level of bidding.

Therefore, the Playing-Trick Test is satisfied.

CONVENTIONS MADE CLOUDY

SOUTH AFRICAN TEXAS: devised by a Boer farmer, a bridge fanatic who lost his bullocks at Rubbabrig on his way to the Outspan Teams Trials. Having disgraced his family, he emigrated to the New World and settled in Texas, ambitious to become an oil baron or get a part in Dallas. Whilst transferring his Krugerands into dollars, he conceived the idea of transferring minor suits into majors; thus a response of 4♣ to partner's opening 1NT requested opener to rebid 4♡. This inspired his partner and compatriot Christian Barnard, who became so keen on heart transfers that he took it up as the profession for which he was cut out.

Intensive care is essential, because this 4♣ bid rules out using it to ask for Aces. This causes loss of Gerber and, when accompanied by lapse of memory, leads to complications such as head shaking and partnership termination.

David Lawton

SERENDIPITY

by Maureen Dennison

This might seem an odd title for an autobiography, but somehow that seems to be the most important aspect of my life.

I was born well before the War – in a year I don't wish to acknowledge, but I was first eligible to play in the Saga with a 60-year-old partner in 1982! My education was minimal: a French Convent with no science or chemistry or higher maths or anything else that is deemed to be of vital importance these days, and even that was interrupted by evacuation, so three years were spent in a little school with one teacher which was part of an artistic community, the home of the Catholic sculptor Eric Gill.

My father wrote books about horse-racing and my first job was as his secretary, which meant a good number of days a year on racecourses – flat racing only, so even the weather was on my side.

I met my husband by chance when he was celebrating his demobilisation and we are fast approaching our 40th anniversary. Our main hobbies are rifle (target) shooting and rallying – with me as the navigator. There were many weekends when he spent Saturday night in the car and Sunday on the ranges: good practice in stamina for championships!

So where did bridge start? When I was a child the whole family used to play kitchen-bridge, so we all learned from the age of seven. I played a little club rubber with my mother after I got married. When my two children had both started school I started a part-time job, later full-time, with the British Market Research Bureau, and two people joined the company, who altered my life: John Samuels and Pat Wolfe. The latter suggested that the company should put a team in for the Great West Road League – DIVISION FIVE! – and he swept half a dozen of us to bridge lessons. I have played with John ever since and in collaboration with him produced *Acol Bidding Made Easy* and, about to be published, *Conventional Bidding Made Easy* which makes use of Decision Trees and flow charts to make each bidding situation clear.

In 1975 I changed my job and became a rep. for a timber & builder's merchant – one of the very few women in the building industry. Then came the next fortuitous event. John and I qualified for the Surrey County Pairs and John had to withdraw. Diana Williams was in the same boat and the County Secretary suggested that we might like to play together. We did, and we got on famously, and that led four years later to our selection for the Common Market Championships in Salsomaggiore, Italy, and the CM, European, and Venice Cup in 1981 which earned four gold medals for Great Britain. We also played in 1983, but only achieved bronze in the European.

Soon after, Diana moved and we broke up as a serious partnership, although we still play three or four times a year. One of our annual outings is the Welsh Ladies Teams playing in tandem with Diana's mother, Margaret Warburton, and we have had a couple of wins there. I have had two winning outings for England in the Lady Milne, in Northern Ireland with Diana, and in Scotland with Fiona Brickwood, with whom I had a regular partnership, twice winning the English National Women's Teams.

So how did I come to be a journalist? Fiona and I made up a scratch team with the late Joe Amsbury and a nice lady called Ena Devres, and she said: "Why don't you write a column for your local paper?" And I thought, why not? So I did, and it was accepted, and *Bridge International*, now *Bridge*, liked my style and now most months I report for them. This gives added interest to any events I play, opportunity to talk to the best players and get hands from them, but also the not-so-great bring me interesting or amusing hands – which makes me feel that every bridge player is my friend.

At about the same time I took my teacher's exams and started local authority teaching. Also around then I was at the Chiltern Congress, sounding off about the organisation of bridge in Britain, and Keith Stanley (then Chairman of the E.B.U.) said: "You should be on the Tournament Committee!" – and that's how I came to be part of the Establishment, though I hope I still keep the views of the ordinary player to the fore.

I gave up full-time work four years ago, and since then my life seems to get fuller and fuller – bridge events here and abroad; two trips to Sicily as a journalist for the Super Bowl; Better Bridge in Britain; helping with the first two B.B.L. Junior Camps; teaching; coaching; writing, and indulging in my other passion: puzzles (a wonderful monthly called *Tough Puzzles*), crosswords and jigsaws (in my household I am given jigsaws, 2000 and up with the picture covered and *no edge pieces*!).

However did I find time to work!

SOLUTIONS TO TEST ON PAGE 67

PROBLEM 1: The best line is to play low from dummy. If North has the ♡A his next play gives it. If South has the ♡A we still have a free heart finesse followed by a diamond finesse.
PROBLEM 2: If the hearts are not worse than 4–2, there is no problem. Since we can hardly cash the ◊A and play for a red-suit squeeze (well against the odds), the best is to cash all the trumps but one and the clubs, reducing dummy to ♡A-K-Q-x-x and ◊A. Then try ♡A-K-Q; if all follow to the second heart, ruff the fourth round. If hearts are 5–1, the only hope is that the same defender started with ◊K which must now drop under the Ace.
PROBLEM 3: Play a low diamond from hand at trick 2. If diamonds are 3–2 and West has the Ace, he must play low. Now switch to clubs, covering East's card for safety, in case clubs are K-Q-9 with East.
PROBLEM 4: Eliminate clubs, draw trumps, cash the ◊A-K, and exit with a diamond. A defender must now give a ruff-and-discard or open up the spades.

121

SOME TERMINOLOGY EXPLAINED

by Amanda Hawthorn

All sports and games have their own language, and bridge is no exception to this. Some of the terms freely bandied about the bridge table can be highly confusing for less-experienced players, and I hope that the following explanation of some of the commonest expressions may be helpful.

Let's take first of all the term *Limit Bid*. These bids are widely used in Acol and, indeed, should always be selected in preference to an *unlimited* bid when appropriate. All bids of no-trumps are limit bids, whether as openings, responses, rebids, or overcalls, in that they carry a definite point range and show a generally balanced hand. So, too, are immediate raises of partner's suit. An unlimited bid is a wide-ranging call and does not promise any specific distribution. An example would be a simple change of suit at the one level, e.g. 1♣ – 1♠. The spade bidder, not having previously passed, might have anything from four or more spades, and five or more points, even as high as twenty on certain hands.

Now what about the expressions *Forcing* and *Invitational?* A forcing bid is made in circumstances when both players accept that the partner of the player who has made it *must* bid at least once more. The simplest example is when a new suit is introduced at the 3-level and no agreement has been reached. 1♠ – 2◊ – 3♡, for instance, and 3♡ is unconditionally forcing. An invitational bid is just what it says it is: "Partner dear, can you bid on?" 1♠ – 2◊ – 2♠ – 3♠, for instance, and 3♠ can (and usually should be!) passed. All conventional bids and cue-bids are forcing, because they do not carry a natural meaning.

Next we come to the expressions *Tolerance* and *Support*. To say that a player has support for a suit means that he guarantees at least three cards opposite partner's five, and four opposite partner's four. Conversely, tolerance implies at least three cards opposite partner's four, or two opposite partner's five. Suppose a player makes a take-out double of an opponent's opening bid which forces his partner to respond. If he only has a moderate hand and is going to accept partner's choice of suit, he guarantees tolerance for each of the three unbid suits, i.e. at least three cards in each. (Of course, if doubler has a very strong hand on which he intends to bid on, he does not always have tolerance for all the unbid suits.) A good example of showing tolerance occurs in the Hackett Defence to Weak-Two opening bids. After an opening of, say, 2♠, the defender who comes into the bidding with 3♣ (a take-out bid showing 12–15 points) shows a principal interest in hearts, with a tolerance for both diamonds and clubs, so that his partner can actually pass 3♣ if that is his own suit, knowing that there is a minumum three-card holding facing him.

The expressions *Simple Preference* and *Jump Preference* often confuse some players. Simple preference can be shown by passing your partner's last bid, or by returning him – at the minimum level – to an earlier suit bid by him. In neither case is any actual support (or in some cases even a tolerance) guaranteed. You hold:

♠ 9 4
♡ K 4
♢ A J 9 8 7
♣ 8 7 6 3

Partner opens 1♠, and you bid 2♢. Partner now tries 2♡. You just give him simple preference back to 2♠. (Don't be tempted to leave him in 2♡ because of the ♡K. You *know* he has five spades, but he has not guaranteed five hearts.)

Move your ♣3 and make it the ♡3. Now you want to play in hearts, in the certain 4–3 (at least) fit, so you give simple preference by passing (unless you prefer to give false preference by bidding 2♠). Now picture yourself holding:

♠ K J 10 2
♡ K J 6
♢ K 8 7 4
♣ 9 2

This time partner opens 1♡ and you bid 1♠. He replies 2♣. Don't be tempted to bid 2NT. You should give jump preference to his hearts by bidding 3♡.

You know partner has five of them and you want him to go on to the heart game unless he has opened on a sub-minimum hand when you would prefer him to pass! Another common phrase used very often to describe these sorts of hands is *Delayed Game Raise*. You hold:

♠ A K 8 7 4
♡ Q J 9 7
♢ K 8
♣ 8 5

Partner opens in front of you with 1♡. If you jump directly to 4♡ you can often miss a slam, so you bid 1♠ and await partner's rebid. If he bids, say, 2♣, now you complete your raise to game by going directly to 4♡.

If he rebids 3♣, then do not complete your delayed game raise. By bidding 4♡ in this sequence you would be denying values for slam and partner would be most likely to pass. A 3♡ bid is now recommended.

Has your partner ever said plaintively when you have just gone two down doubled in 4♠ (all to save a 4♡ contract the other way, which isn't even on): "Mine was only a *competitive* bid – I wasn't really raising you?" Well, the auction has gone:

North	East	South	West
1♡	1♠	3♡	3♠
4♡	4♠	Dbl	All Pass

East, who made the original overcall of 1♠, takes his partner's 3♠ as a free and encouraging bid, and goes to 4♠ thinking he has a real play for it.

♠ 9 8 7
♡ A 10 4 3
♢ Q 9 7 5
♣ J 4

When West puts down this hand, East is horrified, but all West was doing was competing with 3♡ and wanting to push the other side into 4♡ – which he hoped to defeat.

East must bid on only as a deliberate sacrifice. West has other ways of making forward-going bids in this sort of auction.

FIGURE

by Gustavu Aglione

At the lower levels of the bridge galaxy where I play, most of us try to enjoy our game of bridge with a minumum of additional activity as regards concentration and physical or psychological effort. We smoke like chimneys, conversation is always to the fore, and we ruin our bodies by sitting in the wrong posture on backbreaking chairs. And boy, that makes us ugly . . . Fortunately, there are some exceptions to this pattern, and three of them are sitting at my table tonight.

First, of course, there is Galina. Her beauty is so breathtaking that I do not try to describe it. Perhaps it is sufficient to say that Galina is not only my bridge partner, but also the best thing that happened to me in my life. Then, on my right, there is my favourite opponent, Freya. She is a big blonde, whose appearance is such that I quite often wander away in dreams that I do not dare reproduce in writing – yes, sometimes right in the middle of playing a hand. Fortunately for me, usually Dame Fortune takes over and brings the contract which I am playing to an incredibly lucky end.

It is amazing how many beautiful women one can meet at the bridge table, and how few handsome men play the game. Mario on my left is the exception that proves the rule. Freya is partnering him – not the other way round. Women like Galina and Freya choose before they can be chosen . . .

At the end of our session I pick up this hand:

♠ A Q 3 2
♡ J 7 5
♢ A K
♣ A K Q 2

As South, I am the dealer, they are vulnerable and we are not. We play the Multi, so I start with 2♢. After a 'no bid' on my left, Galina puts up the barrage with 3♠.

With this bid she indicates her willingness to play in 4♡ if my Multi is based upon hearts, and to rest in 3♠ if I have a Weak Two in spades. Unfortunately, I do not have a weak Two, but the 23–24 no-trump which is also a part of our Multi. Really, I love those shut-out bids, especially when they are used against partner. Well, everything must have its drawbacks, even the Multi . . . I am not going to spend much time on this. The practical bid has to be 6NT, so that's what I firmly say and everybody passes. Dummy puts down her hand, and I am looking at the cards below.

West leads the ♠J. Well, this looks all right. If the hearts behave, I have twelve easy tricks in a very reasonable contract. If the hearts are 3–3 I have a 75% chance of success, while with the hearts 4–2 the chances are hardly smaller. In both cases, I like to lead the suit from my hand. So I take the ♠J with the King, play a small club to the Ace and see that West is void in this suit, since he discards a diamond. We are lucky that we are not good enough to reach the better 6♣ contract!

Galina
♠ K
♡ A 10 9 6
♢ 9 8 4 2
♣ J 8 6 5

Me
♠ A Q 3 2
♡ J 7 5
♢ A K
♣ A K Q 2

I might need the finesse against the ♡8 later on, so I lead the ♡7 to dummy's ♡9, which to my surprise holds, Mario (West) playing the ♡2 and Freya (East) contributing the ♡3. Now my twelve tricks are certain: three hearts, three spades, two diamonds, and four clubs. Hardly an interesting hand. It is just a matter of losing a trick to Mario's ♡K or ♡Q, and subsequently finessing against his second heart honour. Concentration wanes – with such easy hands one tends to let one's thoughts wander, and with Galina and Freya around daydreaming can be very absorbing.

With an effort, I return to the hand. At trick four, I play a small heart from dummy to Freya's 4 and my Jack. Mario takes this trick with the King and exits with the ♠10 to my Ace. I can repeat the heart finesse now, but in my dream-like trance I prefer to take the easy route: I cash my ♣Q (West discarding a small spade) and the ♣K (West discarding a small diamond). Finally my small club to the Jack seems to give West big trouble. After some thinking, he reluctantly plays the ♡8. So Mario did have the ♡K-Q-8-2, and Freya the ♡4-3. That makes handling the heart suit easier. I play a diamond to my Ace, lead the ♡5, and see that West is now void in the suit!

In the East chair Freya had something really smart cooking: the ♡Q was with her after all! Imagine what would have happened if I had not been so lazy and half-asleep: I would have taken the 'sure' finesse for the ♡Q *before* cashing my four club tricks, and I would have gone down!

It takes some time and a lot of noise before everybody is aware of what is happening. Poor Freya, such a great play exposed by such an extraordinary squeeze on partner! She almost shouts at Mario: "Yes, I can see that you are squeezed in spades and diamonds by the last club, but do you really think that Gustavu is aware of that? Just discard the seven of diamonds smoothly, and he will never dream of cashing the Ace-King of diamonds – he will repeat the heart finesse! Oh, you men are so unimaginative!" And she storms away from the table, all male eyes on her.

Would *you* go down in 6NT on the deal opposite? To duck the ♡Q is a piece of master defence, a supreme example of sophisticated deception. Would you not have been taken in? One always is – by a beautiful woman . . .

```
                  Galina
                  ♠ K
                  ♡ A 10 9 6
                  ◊ 9 8 4 2
                  ♣ J 8 6 5
Mario                            Freya
♠ J 10 9 5 4                     ♠ 8 7 6
♡ K 8 2                          ♡ Q 4 3
◊ Q J 7 6 3                      ◊ 10 5
♣ —                              ♣ 10 9 7 4 3
                  Me
                  ♠ A Q 3 2
                  ♡ J 7 5
                  ◊ A K
                  ♣ A K Q 2
```

I LOVE PARIS

by Stephen Gore

Most of us can remember Maurice Chevalier's self-consciously inimitable French accent extolling the beauties of his wonderful native city. And playing in the famous 'Cino del Duca' pairs tournament this year I was, for the tenth time there, enjoying it all again. The standard was to say the least mixed, in a way it would not be in this country where the weaker players assume that an event in which top-class players are competing is not for them. The fact that in France few people seem to bother to complete a convention card (probably because they all, high and low, play the same simple system) and rarely call the Director, may have something to do with it. Inevitably the event was something of a lottery, though hugely enjoyable as well. It all seemed to depend on what the opponents did; everybody bids (and doubles) on tram-tickets, and the defence was often extra-terrestrial, good and bad.

We finished with 52%, not bad for a new partnership, a score not helped by this hand.

Me
♠ A 9 4 2
♡ 8 6 5 2
◇ J 10 6
♣ A 7

Partner opened 1♣, natural. Next opponent bid 1♠ (I began to wonder if there would ever be an uncontested auction for us) and I doubled (Sputnik, to show four hearts and 7+ points). Partner bid 2♠ (forcing and, at least in principle, asking for a spade stop).

All set to show my spade guard, I was disappointed to hear 3♡ on my right. I felt like doubling, but I've been there before: dummy always is revoltingly better than it has any right to be and you end up with an inadequate penalty to compensate for an easy game, or worse. Pass seemed unduly feeble as I wasn't minimum for my double. In the end I bid 3NT, whereupon partner produced 4◇. Of course, my hitherto talkative opponent now passed, just when I might have liked to hear from him again.

What should I bid over 4◇? Partner is presumably at least 5–5, probably 6–5 in the minors. With my two Aces a slam looks possible, so long as the defence cannot take two hearts, or one heart and another trick. I'd like to bid 5♣ to show the Ace, but this sounds like a sign-off; 4♠ might still leave partner worried about the clubs. Finally, I settled for 5◇, in the hope that partner – taking all my previous bids into account – might take this as encouraging. No such luck: partner passed with the hand below.

Partner
♠ —
♡ 3
◇ A K Q 7 5
♣ K Q J 9 8 6 2

Plus 420 did not gain many match points! *Quia culpa?* I think I should have bid 4NT over 4◇, surely not Blackwood but a general slam try with no convenient bid available. Presumably partner would have accepted.

However, I think partner was thrice pessimistic, first in not opening with a strong bid, second in bidding 2♠ instead of 4◇, and third in not punting a slam over my 5◇. Admittedly, he was worried about the ♣A – but he also knew that I had no way of showing it as a slam try. What do *you* think?

WHAT'S LURKING? (*page 22*)

The ten Bridge Coups illustrated are Alcatraz, Bath, Crocodile, Deschapelles, Devil's, Morton's Fork, Scissors, Trump, Grand, Merrimac.

FLEMING'S GIANT CROSSWORD (*pages 84-85*)

Across: 1 Precision Club System, 13 Hostage, 14 Tench, 15 Burster, 16 Staging-post, 17 Leukaemia, 18 Hit-men, 19 Costate, 20 Plushy, 23 Overspent, 25 Throwing off, 30 Russophobia, 32 Beech-mast, 34 Cocker, 36 Amomums, 37 Sparti, 41 Notorious, 42 Northerlies, 43 Apricot, 44 Enrol, 45 Realise, 46 Philadelphia Lawyers.

Down: 2 Restart, 3 Chariness, 4 Sleigh, 5 Orthodontic, 6 Constitutional Monarch, 7 Upholster, 8 Subdue, 9 Streamlined, 10 Entombs, 11 The School for Scandal, 12 Treaty of Westminster, 21 Lengthy, 22 Swooned, 24 Ewers, 26 Osaka, 28 Isometrical, 29 Subumbrella. 31 Bombshell, 33 Hypergamy, 35 Catarrh, 38 Rainier, 39 Sorted, 40 Thoria.

SPOT THE DIFFERENCES (*page 95*)

1. The pack of cards held by the player facing you.
2. Her hairslide.
3 & 4. Her cuffs.
5. The neck of the sweater worn by the player on the right.
6. The legs of the chair on which he is sitting.
7. The pocket on the jacket of the player seen from the back.
8. The next player's tie.
9 & 10. His trouser turn-ups.

BRIDGE TRIVIA QUIZ (*page 105*)

1. Charles Goren.
2. Iain Macleod.
3. Victor Mollo.
4. Taiwanese (C.C. Wei).
5. Double no Aces, Pass 1 Ace; Redouble no Aces, Pass 1 Ace.
6. To the name of the road in Hampstead where the club, in which the system was formulated, was situated.
7. Helen Sobel.
8. Benito Garozzo and Leon Yallouse.
9. Hearts.
10. N.p.c. Carlo Alberto Perroux, Walter Avarelli, Giorgio Belladonna, Camillo Pabis Ticci, Massimo d'Alelio, Pietro Forquet, Benito Garozzo.
11. Cornelius Ryan.
12. In Venice – linking the Doge's Palace to the State Prison.

JOIN THE DOTS (*page 114*)

A Bridge!

EPILOGUE
by Elena Jeronimidis

Many people, when picking up a book, open it at the last page. If you are one of them, you will be disappointed to find that no world-shaking climax is reached here. To me, this page marks the end of a busy time spent editing all the contributions which have made these last months so exciting. I am nothing but sad to part with the result of our labours, yet I hope that when THE BRIDGE PLUS ANNUAL is in your hands, you will find it the good read which we aimed to produce and will enjoy and treasure it as much as I do.

One way of coping with the sadness of reaching the end of an absorbing task is to thank all those who shared it. If our new Annual is successful, then the credit must first go to the authors. From professionals to amateurs, from top players to novices, they all equally contributed to sustaining my enthusiasm and I am very grateful to them for making my own work so pleasurable. Their names are listed on the back cover, together with those of the artists and the many people who have helped in the production of this book.

However, special thanks must go to John Magee for providing unfailing support and many stimulating discussions; Brian Best for his advice, as well as willingness to try out new ideas; David Barnes, Dennis Cook, and Roger Trowell for reading the manuscript; Eric Crowhurst for checking the technical content. Last, but by no means least, Andrew Parker for much constructive criticism.